The Visual Squash An NL

NLP Mast

By Jess Marion and Shawn Carson

Changing Mind Publishing

New York, NY

The Visual Squash: An NLP Tool for Radical Change
NLP Mastery Series
Copyright 2013 Shawn Carson, Jess Marion and Changing Minds Publishing. All rights reserved.
Cover design by Richie Williams
Photography by Caroline Berghonzi
Editing by Nancy Rawlinson
No part of this book may be reproduced in any manner whatsoever without written permission except in the case of brief quotations embedded in critical articles and reviews. For further information please contact Changing Mind Publishing at 545 8th Avenue, Suite 930, New York, NY, 10001.

Table of Contents

Foreword *5*

Chapters:

    1) Welcome to the Visual Squash *7*

    2) The Classic Visual Squash in Action *14*

    3) The Neuroscience of the Visual Squash *22*

    4) How the Squash Works *25*

    5) Catalepsy *37*

    6) Chunking Up *47*

    7) Reintegration *63*

    8) Deep Trance Reintegration *80*

    9) The Content-Free Squash *99*

    10) The Conversational Squash *105*

    11) The NLP Negotiation Pattern *120*

    12) Self-Reintegration *130*

13) Conclusion *140*

Appendix *142*

About the Authors *147*

Acknowledgements *148*

Glossary *149*

Other Publications *151*

Foreword

This book dives deep into one of my favorite NLP patterns. I teach this process in my classes because it encapsulates many of the most important principles behind good change work. Knowing the authors, as I do, I expected a well thought out and presented overview and breakdown of the visual squash and all it's variations. This book exceeded those expectations in so many ways and on so many levels.

Yes, they deliver the most comprehensive treatment of this pattern that I've ever read, and believe, has ever been written. But, even better, they use this platform to cover the most crucial elements of lasting, generative change that goes way beyond the pattern and into the very nature of change itself.

In this book you will learn a complex system that aligns all levels of experience from the behavioral up to identity, covering and uncovering the values, beliefs and unconscious motivations behind the problems and, more importantly, the solutions. Shawn and Jess make sure to give you many different ways of adapting this process to fit any client in any context. From a purely conversational approach more appropriate for a business coach to a deep trance variation perfect for a hypnosis session, you are guaranteed to find useful ways of implementing these ideas.

The authors also cover some key linguistic concepts, from temporal and spatial predicates to the whys and hows of addressing nominalizations. This is learning that changes every aspect of the therapeutic/coaching interaction by teaching multi level communication that speaks directly to the unconscious mind. And this, in my opinion, changes everything.

Having nearly completed a book on the neuroscience of change with Shawn Carson, I was excited to see the neural underpinnings of the Visual Squash included here. I agree with the authors that understanding the basics of neuroplasticity and hemispheric specialization allow for a more thorough integration. It also gives the practitioner a different way of understanding and utilizing this pattern that works with the natural way the brain learns and processes. This is vital information for changing minds.

The chapter on arm catalepsy should be required reading for anyone using hypnosis or deep coaching with their clients. It is one the best and simplest descriptions I've come across and even shows you how to use it for yourself. This book teaches an easy, yet powerful self- hypnosis technique that is sure to give the reader an experience of trance that goes way beyond simple guided imagery and visualization.

The Visual Squash, as presented by the authors, is a truly comprehensive form of parts integration that generates resources that stay with the client long after the specific changes are made. The content free version allows clients to address issues they might not be ready or willing to share, creating a safe space for healing and transformation.

When I first heard about this mastery series I thought it was a good idea. After reading the first two books, I realize it's not really a good idea at all. It's a great one. I'm envisioning this series as playing a vital role in not just NLP training, but in any training in the coaching and mental health field. This series will be required reading for both my coaching and hypnosis students because I couldn't have taught this better myself. Shawn and Jess are onto something big here. They have provided a way to fill a gap in our learning we didn't even realize we had. And I'm already excited to read the next one.
Enjoy!

Melissa Tiers

Author of "Integrative Hypnosis: A Comprehensive Course in Change" and "The Anti-Anxiety Toolkit: Rapid Techniques to Rewire your Brain"

Chapter One: Welcome to the Visual Squash

Neuro-Linguistic Programming — NLP — is all about helping clients to change. Even when handling simple problems, part of your client wants to make a change (otherwise they would not be in your office), while another part wants to maintain the existing pattern of behavior or feeling (otherwise they would have already changed). Clients are often "of two minds" in this way. In NLP, we talk about conflicting "parts." As a coach, you can use the idea of conflicting parts to understand most problems and there's an NLP pattern, the Visual Squash, which specifically addresses this kind of conflict. The Visual Squash, a type of parts reintegration, is one of the most powerful tools we have in NLP to create lasting change in clients.

It is important to understand that each part of the client is motivated by a positive intention. If you think about it, it would run counter to our own survival as a species if people acted in ways that were not beneficial to them. That does not mean that every behavior we engage in is healthy, useful, or even beneficial — at least, not on the *surface*. But if you dig deeper, you can discover positive intentions behind even seemingly dysfunctional behaviors. For example, if you have a client who is a smoker and wants to quit, the part of them that wants to quit clearly has positive intentions: this part might want to keep them healthy, give them access to more money, or make sure they have a longer life. But what about the positive intention behind the seemingly negative smoking behavior itself? Well, for some smokers it may be the opportunity to relax and escape stress; for others, perhaps it's a chance to socialize and have a break at work. So while the behavior itself is not beneficial, on a deeper level it is meeting some very important need of the client. If you want to help your client to change, you must make sure that those hidden needs are met in new ways because, if not, then the problem behavior will recur, or the client will substitute some other behavior that may also be destructive.

Human beings are proficient at meeting their own needs. In NLP, we say people work perfectly. We do what we need to ensure we have the most desirable outcome. Because we work "perfectly," creating change can be easy, quick, and natural. Both you and your client have every resource necessary to create positive and lasting change in the client's life. The first step, though, is understanding that all parts of the client must be engaged in the process of change. In fact, when all parts are working together, the issue resolves itself.

Problems arise when a client wants two seemingly contradictory things at the same time, or when he both wants and doesn't want something. Until this happens the client does not have a problem in the way we use the term, meaning a problem for them. If, for example, a smoker comes into your office, and you ask him why he want to quit smoking and he says, "Because my wife wants me to," or "My doctor ordered me to," you may not want to take him on as a client; the problem is not an issue for him and he does not have a strong enough conflict with his smoking. It is certainly a problem for his wife or doctor, but for him, on a deep level, it is not an issue. Clients who do not have conflict between different parts inside of them are not yet ready to change. We are looking for the emotional connection between the client's problem and their desire to change. Their desire for change is the fuel that will propel them forward in this process and it will make clear that the conflicting parts are ready to be reintegrated.

It is often very easy to identify problems that involve conflicting parts because the client will tell you! They may say, "On one hand I want to do this and on the other hand I want to do that." Or they may say, "I want to do this but don't want to do that." They may also nonverbally indicate that they have conflicting parts by gesturing toward one side of the body when speaking about what they want and gesturing to the other side when speaking about what they don't want.

However, the client may not always make the conflicting

parts clear. In these cases you need to listen for descriptions of what they want and what has stopped them thus far. For example, you may have a client who wants to pursue a new career. They may say something like, "I really want to follow my dreams but each time I think about leaving my current job, I get anxious so I don't take action." In fact, the only type of coaching problem that cannot be described as a parts conflict is where the client wants something but simply does not have the resources to get it, "I want to give a recital but I don't know if I can…" In order to clarify the type of issue, you can ask, "How is this behavior a problem for you?" or, "What stops you from achieving that goal?" Once the parts are clarified in your mind, you can point out the parts to the client, perhaps by saying something like, "So on the one hand you want to quit your current job to pursue your dreams, but on the other hand you enjoy the safety and security of your current job. Is that right?" The question at the end is important, because it gives the client the space to either agree or, if she feels the parts are not accurately described, correct you.

You can use the Visual Squash in a variety of situations, but now we will consider the ones that occur the most frequently.

Toward-Toward and Toward-Away Conflicts

What we call a *toward-toward* conflict is when the client would like two different and seemingly mutually exclusive things at the same time. For example, a client may want to quit his job to pursue other interests, but also want to stay in his current safe, secure job. This is a choice between two possible options, each of which has benefits and drawbacks. The client is essentially saying, "I want both of these options at the same time, but they are mutually exclusive. I can't have both!" The coaching strategy is to help the client find a way to have the *benefits* of both options at the same time. This could mean working two jobs at once, but more likely it will mean finding a way to meet the emotional needs both options would fulfill for the client. This type of conflict arises when the client has two different parts both vying for his time and energy.

The *toward-away* conflict arises when a client would like a particular outcome but not want something else that goes along with it. An example is a client who would like to lose weight but hates to exercise. On one hand they want to lose the weight while on the other hand they don't want to go to the gym. In this toward-away conflict, the "away" is holding the client back from reaching the "toward" goal.

In both varieties of conflict the client is caught in the middle, unable to congruently move in either direction, and so the conflict persists. There is a third type conflict we will mention only briefly. On a very rare occasion you may have a client with and Away-Away conflict. An example of this would be the weight loss client who says they don't want to be fat and they don't want to exercise. With this type of conflict you could help the client get clarity on their values in order to change one or both of the away values into toward values. In NLP, this is called a "values elicitation and clean up"and the detail of how to perform it is outside the scope of this book.

Secondary Gain

Another type of issue the Visual Squash is perfect for is that which arises from secondary gain. Secondary gain is the hidden benefit that the client experiences from the problem state or behavior. Because there *is* a hidden benefit (hidden, at least, from the client's conscious mind), the client's unconscious mind maintains the conflict because it is getting something of value out of it. The benefit of maintaining the problem is greater than the benefit of changing, at least as far as the unconscious mind is concerned. This is still a toward-toward, or toward-away from conflict, but it operates at the unconscious level. You could think of the client who has a fear of driving. They want to feel comfortable driving but by *not* driving, they get the pay off of not having to take their kids to school, and always having someone else drive them around, and so on. The secondary gain here is that by not driving, the client doesn't have to be responsible for certain things. This would be a toward-away conflict and the secondary gain is powerful enough to continue the problem.

Every problem has some level of secondary gain in it. This manifests as a parts conflict. If it did not, there would be no reason for it to continue. Think about your clients and the problems that they bring into your office. You can be curious about the gains they are benefiting from by maintaining those problems. The woman with agoraphobia who is afraid to leave her home, does not have to go outside to do chores; she does not have to go to the store or pick up her kids from school. Everyone else has been doing these things for her, and coming round to visit her. Why give up the fear in her mind when she is benefiting by not having to leave the house? You don't have to know exactly what the secondary gain is when you start working with the client, just that it is there and can be thought of as a part that is in conflict with the client's goals. The secondary gain may resolve on its own if the unconscious mind learns new strategies that allow its needs to be met in a healthier way, but it's more common for secondary gain to become an issue that must be addressed directly.

There are some very easy ways to spot secondary gain conflicts that may be interfering with the change process. The first is when you have a client who, during the initial coaching program, reaches their goal. Then they return a few weeks, months, or years later with the same issue. Clearly, the needs that their problem behavior was addressing are still not being met. You may encounter this with smokers who have quit in the past, only to return to the habit, maybe saying that they started again because they felt stressed. This is a strong indicator that the client has not developed healthier ways of coping with stress. They do not yet have access to greater calmness, relaxation, or the other positive resources that they need to make it through a stressful situation.

Another indicator of secondary gain issues can arise when the client has achieved her goal, but a new problem has developed. This is sometimes called "symptom substitution" because the client is replacing one problem with another; each is a symptom of a deeper need. For example, a smoker may quit smoking but then develop a weight problem. She has replaced smoking with overeating. This shows that whatever need the smoking was meeting for her has not been met in other ways, so she has replaced the cigarettes with food. This is why you so often hear of smokers wanting to quit but being afraid that they will gain weight. We will go into the ways to reframe those beliefs later in the book.

So how do you identify and address a secondary gains issue? The first step is to listen closely to what your client is telling you, because she will unconsciously indicate a parts conflict or a secondary gain issue through the type of words that she uses, as well as her nonverbal communication, her body language, her tonality, and so on. You could think of the client who comes in and has a case of the exclusive "ors". This means that they believe their choice is mutually exclusive: "I could relax or go to the gym." Anytime a client is limiting themselves through exclusive ors or negation, for example using "but" — "I could stop smoking but I enjoy it" — you have a strong indicator of a secondary gain issue.

It is also important to re-evaluate the problem each step of the way with each new piece of information that the client gives you during the change process, and after each intervention, whether you were using an NLP pattern, hypnosis, or something else. All new information changes the problem in one way or another. Change may be small or great, which is why testing and re-evaluation are so important in order to see where the client is, along the path of transformation.

We can also re-evaluate by future pacing, that is simply orienting the client to a future time and place and having them experience accessing the resources they have developed as a result of the change. When the client steps into the future they begin to build a future memory of what it will be like to accomplish their goal and their commitment to themselves is reinforced. If the client appears to have made a change, but then experiences a block during the testing or future pacing portion of the session, it could point to a secondary gain issue, which you can address through the use of a Visual Squash. For example, if we work with the reluctant driver, and as a result they seem very confident imagining being behind the wheel, but when we ask them to imagine driving to the grocery store, then to pick up the kids from school, they back off the change they have made. This may indicate they have developed a "confident driver" part, but the part that enjoys other people doing things for them is blocking their transformation.

In short, the Visual Squash is suitable for nearly any client issue because all problems have an element of secondary gain, as well as a toward-toward or toward-away structure. The Visual Squash pattern uses a wonderful combination of imagery, catalepsy (a balancing of the muscles that indicates an unconscious process is taking place, which we will discuss fully later in the book), and unconscious logic to create positive change. All three of these states are part of a trance experience. The pattern can be done in a way that appears to be more uptime or conscious, which is valuable in situations where formal hypnosis would not be appropriate. And it can also be done in a way that is far more overtly hypnotic. Either way, because you are eliciting unconscious material through the use of symbols as well as catalepsy, you can rest assured that the unconscious mind is fully engaged in the process of change, and the client is experiencing some level of trance, which is useful to you as the coach and is also useful for the client. After all, all learning happens in trance. Trance allows the moving of information from conscious awareness to implicit memory. Without trance learning does not happen.

In the rest of this book, we will explore the many ways in which you can use the Visual Squash and Reintegration to create powerful, lasting change. We will begin by breaking down the process so you can have a step-by-step understanding of how to do the classic NLP Visual Squash. We will then present alternative versions including a deep trance and a conversational Visual Squash. Finally, we will present two contexts outside of the coaching field in which you can apply this technique: in business and for your own self-coaching. Our goal is to help you develop a deeper understanding of this pattern and also to help you experiment with new ways of applying this pattern in various parts of your life.

Receive your book bonus at www.visualsquashbookbonus.com

Chapter Two: The Classic Visual Squash in Action

Before we explore the mechanics of this pattern, let's take a few moments to examine the Visual Squash in action. This example involves a client who felt that he was at a point of transition in his professional life. This client enjoyed two different kinds of work and felt competition between these areas of his life. Part of him wanted one thing while another part wanted something different.

Coach: What would you like to work through today?

Client: I'm torn between continuing my consulting work and leaving to pursue my writing.

Coach: OK, so it's like you're being pulled in two different directions.

Client: Yes.

Coach: On one hand you want to continue your work and on the other pursue the writing.

Client: Right.

Coach: So, I'm curious: this part of you that wants to continue on with the consulting work, what is it doing for you? What are you getting out of it?

Client: It's more lucrative, so there's money involved. Money lets me pay my rent, pay my bills. The work is interesting and I enjoy it and it gives me a sense of security, of knowing I can go back to it full-time if I need to. Oh, and there's something else as well: it's not quite a status thing, but it's knowing I'm a part of the wider world.

Coach: All right. And when you think about the side of you that wants to pursue the writing? What is that doing for you?

Client: It's growth and fulfillment.

Coach: Excellent. So you have two sides wanting to go in seemingly opposite directions. It may be more useful to you to have both parts working together. Does that sound good to you?

Client: Yes, that would be good!

Coach: Great. Is it OK if I touch your hands?

Client: Mmm-hmm.

Coach: I'm going to pick up this arm [lifts client's right hand]. If this arm were to represent either the side of you that wants to continue consulting or the side that wants to pursue writing, which would it be?

Client: Hmm, the consulting side.

Coach: That's right, the consulting side. This hand then is the writing side [lifts the client's left arm].

Client: Yes.

Coach: So as you look at the side that wants to write, I'm curious what would represent this. If you could give it a symbol to represent wanting to write, what would it be?

Client: It's a quill, a quill pen.

Coach: And what about this side that wants to keep consulting? [Points to right hand.] What symbol comes to mind?

Client: I see myself in a suit.

Coach: Yourself in a suit.

Client: Mmm-hmm.

Coach: Yourself in a suit there and the quill over here [points to each hand]. So I'm curious: what does this side want for you [touches left hand], because both parts of you want something positive? If you were to consider this quill here writing, what does it want for you?

Client: It's personal growth and something about a flower.

Coach: Personal growth, flower, and even above those, who will you be as a person?

Client: I'll be somebody who is on top.

Coach: Somebody who is on top. And when you're on top, what does that do for you?

Client: I can see a long way.

Coach: And how does it feel when you can see a long way?

Client: It feels good.

Coach: That's right, it feels good. And even beyond feeling good, who are you from the top, having that growth?

Client: I'm myself.

Coach: Yourself.

Client: Yes.

Coach: That's right. This part that would like to continue with the consulting, you there in the suit, what does this side want for you?

Client: Um, there's safety.

Coach: Safety.

Client: Yeah, almost a conformity.

Coach: And beyond the safety and conformity, what else?

Client: It's keeping me from being alone.

Coach: And when you're not alone, what are you?

Client: With other people.

Coach: And what does that do for you?

Client: It lets me fit in.

Coach: And when you're not alone and you're fitting in, how do you feel?

Client: It's almost like it doesn't want me to find out who I am. Isn't that funny?

Coach: Isn't that funny. What may happen when you find out who you are?

Client: I guess that's what it doesn't want me to find out.

Coach: And in that not wanting to find out, that not being alone, that safety, that's right [coach notices trance responses]. I wonder what this hand can tell you about the not wanting to find out? Because I'm starting to think that you have two different parts at work here. It isn't the consulting and the writing; it's the not wanting to find out who you are and the wanting to discover who you are. How does it feel to consider that?

Client: This one seems very constraining [touches right hand, the side that doesn't want to know].

Coach: It is constraining, and what is it doing for you?

Client: Oh, it's giving me a path.

Coach: It's giving you a path.

Client: Yeah.

Coach: And when you have that path, how does it feel?

Client: It feels like I know where I'm going.

Coach: And what is that experience like?

Client: It's regular — no, routine.

Coach: What does that routine give you?

Client: Um, I'm spinning . . . [Client is doing a transderivational search. He is moving through his different experiences rapidly to find the answer. This is indicated through his eye accessing cues.] Safety.

Coach: What do you get from having that safety?

Client: Oh, I can be myself in other areas.

Coach: You can be yourself in other areas. This part over there that wants you to discover who you are, what is it doing for you?

Client: Self-actualization.

Coach: And when you're self-actualized?

Client: I'm me.

Coach: And how does that feel?

Client: Good [physiological shift].

Coach: Good. When you've taken the path and realized you can be you [points to problem side], how does that feel?

Client: Good [physiological shift].

Coach: You mean both sides want you to feel good?

Client: Yeah.

Coach: So what I would like for you to do is to watch these hands because they have already begun a journey [coach has noticed the client's hands beginning to move together], and eventually in their own time when they do touch, I would like for your unconscious mind to create a new symbol. This new symbol lets you know that both parts are working together because each side of you has something to give the other side. This part of you that will give safety and can let you feel good on that path, it has a skill that it can give this other side to help you discover who you are. What is that skill?

Client: It's like practicality, getting things done.

Coach: Practicality and getting things done. What about this side over here? What skill can it give?

Client: Vision and growth.

Coach: Practicality, getting things done, vision, and growth. [Touches both hands, begins to touch the "wrong" side as she mentions each skill.] And as those hands come together, your unconscious mind prepares that new symbol. Vision and practicality, getting things done, and growth. That's right . . . that's it. And when those hands do touch, that symbol will appear in its own time. That's it. What is that there? [Client's hands touch.] What do you see there?

Client: I see a rope going up like the Indian Rope Trick.

Coach: I'd like for you to take that rope going up and make it a part of who you are in any way that is appropriate for you. Practicality, growth, vision, getting things done — that rope going up represents discovering who you are, following a path, having others around you while discovering who you are. Maybe even a routine way of making discoveries.

[Client smiles.]

Coach: Only when that rope is fully integrated, and all parts of you are working together, can you keep feeling good and practically having vision and growth in a way that gets things done. Now, you can your eyes open and return to the room, with full movement in your arms. In your own time.

[Client begins to emerge from trance.]

Coach: Welcome back. Great work! How do you feel?

Client: I feel good!

Coach: That's right. When you think about discovering who you are, how does that feel?

Client: It's good.

Coach: And writing versus consulting?

Client: I can find out who I am while doing both. The consulting doesn't stop that.

Coach: It doesn't? Are you sure?

Client: Yes.

Coach: How do you know?

Client: Because I feel good!

Coach: And as you are feeling good you can consider sometime soon when you will be writing, knowing that the consulting is there waiting for you. Or perhaps you will be consulting, feeling good knowing that writing is right around the corner

Client: Yes, thank you!

The above transcript is the layout of the Classic Visual Squash with a type of issue that suggests we use the Squash. The coach elicited the parts and the client assigned one to each hand. They then began the process finding the positive intention behind both, allowing both sides to share resources. Finally the parts were integrated and the client had the experience of really knowing that the choices were not mutually exclusive and it could be easy to generate a new and better option. Finally we tested the change and took the client into the future to test it out (future pace).

In the next chapter we will take a look at the Classic Visual Squash in more detail, and, following that, at each part of the Squash separately.

Receive your book bonus at www.visualsquashbookbonus.com

Chapter Three: The Neuroscience of The Visual Squash

The Visual Squash essentially takes an "either-or" dilemma that the client faces and splits it into two choices. So the client might say, "On the one hand I would like to take some time off and travel, but on the other hand I don't want to leave my job..." How does this sort of internal conflict arise? It may be that we simply want two things, "I think I'll have Italian food...or maybe Chinese would be good..." or there are pros and cons to a decision, "That job sounds awesome, but the money isn't so great..."

It's obvious that we can have different neural circuits, each driving us toward a different behavior or feeling. In fact our brains are designed to run numerous conflicting neural networks, and to only act when one of these networks has built up enough steam to generate a coordinated action.

But what about the situations where the dilemma comes to control and define our lives? We become locked into one behavior, but tormented by our inability to pursue another. Or we simply freeze in a state of indecision.

Here we are going to propose a neural mechanism that may explain these long-lasting and seemingly insurmountable dilemmas, based upon brain hemispheres and their specialization. It has long been known that we have a left brain and a right brain separated, or joined perhaps, by a set of neurons called the corpus callosum. The corpus callosum forms a communication bridge between the two hemispheres. Much of our knowledge of brain hemispheres comes from the work of Roger Wolcott Sperry, who received the Nobel Prize for medicine and physiology in 1981 for his work on 'split-brain' patients: people who had their corpus callus severed in order to cure extreme epilepsy.

This severing allowed the two hemispheres to work more independently and allowed Sperry to conduct experiments to determine the preferences, strengths and weaknesses of each hemisphere. Journalists and writers seeking to write intelligible and entertaining explanations for the popular market have exaggerated the findings of these experiments. However it is true that each hemisphere has unique abilities, and presumably its own preferences for life choices. For example, the left brain is more logical and cognitive and is responsible for word choice and word understanding. The right brain processes tonality and other auditory cues, and is more imaginative.

Is it therefore possible that the major dilemmas we face, when we have seemingly incompatible life choices, may be caused by hemispheric disagreement? Is it, literally, "My left brain wants this, but my right brain wants that"? Although there is no way to test or prove such a contention, nevertheless considering either-or dilemmas in this way provides a rich metaphor for both the issue and the solution, and allows us to perform the Visual Squash with more elegance and power.

Many NLP practitioners do the Visual Squash as a more cognitive or left brain pattern. But if the dilemma is not "on the left hand I want this and on the right hand I want that," but rather, "On the left brain I want this and on the right brain I want that," then we can use hemispheric specialization to leverage the power of the Visual Squash.

The Classic Visual Squash is actually a perfect mix of left and right brain activities. We start by doing something verbal — naming the parts — which favors the left brain, then we do something imaginative and visual — creating visual symbols — which favors the right brain. Then we do something else language based by asking, "What does that do for you?" and then something emotional. You can see how the pattern exchanges abilities not just between the parts on the left hand and right hand, but also between the right and left hemispheres of the brain.

This approach allows us to consider this as a disagreement between verbal and visual, literal and symbolic, logical and emotional, and between the preferences and abilities of the left brain and the preferences and abilities of the right brain.

Taking this to its logical and metaphorical conclusion, when performing a Squash you could consciously alternate questions directed to the client's left and right brains. For example, if part of the client wants to stay in their current job and part wants to leave you could ask, "What is the name of the part that wants to stay? What is the name of the part that wants to leave?" That's left-brain activity because we are labeling the parts, and naming is left-brain. And you could be listening for the tonality the client uses when describing the part, and, using that tonality, you could ask, "What's the image representing the part that wants you to stay?" Tonality and imagery are both more right brain activities. Then you could ask, "What is the benefit, the positive intention, of that part?" This is a logical, so left brain, question. But then you ask, "How do you feel about that part?" Feelings are more right brain.

Alternating in this way leads the client's brain to literally fire on both cylinders, and begins the integration of the left and right neural networks responsible for maintaining the parts separately. This will lead to integration of the parts as they begin to wire together across the corpus callosum. The coach can encourage this integration by asking more integrative left *and* right brain questions such as, "What do you feel about that thought? What do you think about that feeling? What's everything else that's not that thought? Please be more specific about that feeling."

Receive your book bonus at www.visualsquashbookbonus.com

Chapter Four: How the Visual Squash Works

Identifying the Parts

The first step in the Visual Squash is to have the client identify the two parts. The parts may become clear as the client is discussing their problem but if not, you can inquire about it, suggesting that it is "like part of you wants [this] and another part wants [that]." Then you wait for their response. They may agree or disagree congruently (i.e., both consciously and unconsciously). Or they may disagree consciously while agreeing unconsciously, or vice versa.

As a coach you should be aware of both the conscious and unconscious communication a client is offering. Consciously they may agree or disagree by saying yes or no, but what is the client's unconscious mind saying? The unconscious mind communicates most directly through body language, gesture, and tonality. You may see this when a client says yes and yet their body shows some sort of incongruity such as a change in breathing, tension in the muscles, body positioning, or color in the face. Even if you do not consciously recognize the two layers of communication occurring, you will have a feeling that something is not quite right. This is because, just as you consciously track conscious communication, you *unconsciously* recognize *unconscious* communication. Your conscious mind has a conversation with their conscious mind, while your unconscious mind has a conversation with their

25

unconscious mind! Trust your unconscious mind: it can make distinctions between multilevel communications while you continue to develop your awareness at the conscious level.

Once the parts are identified, ask if you can touch the client's hands during the course of the work. If they should say no, then go on to the Conversational and Deep Trance Squashes presented later in this book. Assuming they say yes, gently lift the client's hands, ensuring that the elbows are free from any chair, table, or other surface that would block free movement. Now you can suggest that each hand represents one of the parts. You can then have the client assign each hand a specific part. Point to the one hand first and ask the client what part they think that particular hand represents. Then, moving to the second hand, have them confirm that it represents the part that was not yet assigned. You can go back and see how that played out in our example at the end of Chapter One.

The Search for the Symbol

Now you're ready to fully engage with the client's unconscious mind to create positive change. The ways you do this within the Visual Squash are through imagery and through catalepsy. We will explore catalepsy in greater detail in the next chapter. Right now, we will focus specifically on the use of imagery, and how imagery can get the client's conscious and unconscious minds to interact with each other in a new way.

So the stage is set: the conflicting parts are in place and you, as coach, can begin working with each part. How does the client interact with those parts on an unconscious level, in her or his day-to-day life? A key way of discovering this is by assigning a symbol to each of the parts because imagery is a vital part of the human experience. Just as the conscious mind enjoys using words to communicate ideas, the unconscious mind prefers to use images, sensations, and other sensory experiences to communicate. A large portion of the human brain is dedicated specifically to visual processing and therefore using visual symbols activates the unconscious mind. Having the client create a symbol or representation for each of the conflicting parts also helps the client to dissociate from the problem and to see it clearly, in a safe, comfortable way. Distancing the client from the issue gives him or her the space and perspective to be able to address both sides in a way that they have not been able to do before.

These two symbols will be used as indirect indicators of the transformation that takes place throughout this pattern. Having these symbols in place primes the unconscious mind to learn and develop new ways of resolving the conflict, ways that rely on the client's vast store of unconscious inner resources. Be aware that the symbols may spontaneously change as the conflict begins to resolve itself!

Eliciting the symbols is quite easy, but remember that the process of change begins with your own inner state. You, as the coach, need to be bigger than whatever issue the client comes with. If the client senses that their problem is too big for you to handle, or that you are not completely convinced of the efficacy of the pattern, they will pick up on that. If, on the other hand, you come from a place where you are certain that you know just the right path for the client to experience profound change, then that certainty also becomes communicated. When you expect the client to succeed and think to yourself that the client is an incredibly resourceful human being who has every skill that she or he needs in order to create this change, then your client will unconsciously pick up on this and follow suit. This does not mean that you are inflexible, pushing the client to fit into a particular pattern. Rather it is the attitude that you know the client has every resource they need to be successful in this process. Your positive coaching state, together with your hypnotic-language skills, including: language softeners (modal operators of possibility: can, could, perhaps, maybe, etc), and positive presuppositions and assumptions about the client, help to lay the groundwork so that the symbols emerge naturally and spontaneously. Your own state as a coach is paramount: while you assist the client, inside your own mind you must have the expectation that the client is able to generate the symbols unconsciously and easily.

The Process

Begin by gesturing to the hand that represents the least conflicting, most positive, or most energetic part. For example, in the case of a client who wants to change jobs but also wants to stay in his current position (as in the example above), this might be the desire for the new job as long as this part seems to carry a lot of positive energy. It is often the more conflicting, least positive, or least energetic part that is causing the conflict and keeping the client from moving forward. For a client who wants to be successful but is afraid of failure, the least conflicting part would be the success side, and the fear is the part that has been keeping the client from realizing his goal. For a smoker, the more positive side would be the desire to stop smoking, and the more conflicting or negative side would be the one that wants to continue smoking.

Starting with the more positive tends to make the process easier and faster. It's easy to find the positive intention of the positive part and this indirectly prepares the client for finding value and resources in the more troublesome part.

Next, you suggest that the client unconsciously create a symbol for that part and let it appear in their hand. This will be a symbol that they can recognize as representing that specific part of them. What you are doing is asking the client to have a positive visual hallucination, a powerful experience of hypnotic phenomena, even though they do not realize it.

Language softeners are very useful at this point. If you simply tell your client to see a symbol in their hand, it puts a high level of conscious pressure on them, and while some pressure is useful, too much could block the client from having a true unconscious experience. Instead, you need to give a gentle unconscious push to bring that symbol forward. This brings up an important point: we are looking for unconscious involvement here. A consciously constructed symbol will not be as powerful. Your ability to recognize the difference between the unconscious and the conscious hinges upon your ability to pace the client's experience at the unconscious level. You are looking for signs of trance in the form of catalepsy (we will cover this topic in depth in the next chapter). If your client is "normally organized," you may also notice them looking up and to their right, or looking forward with a slightly defocused gaze. This is because the client is accessing the "visual-create" part of their eye accessing cues. Visual-create is where the unconscious power lies. If the client is consciously constructing the symbol, they may look up and to their left (for normally organized), indicating they are more consciously accessing their memories. (Be aware that some people are reversed organized, so they access visual-create to the left and not the right.)

When the symbol is consciously constructed, it may look

like the actual resource or problem. For example, a client who wants to lose weight might make a picture of herself skinny (for the part that wants to lose weight), and another picture of herself eating (for the part that enjoys comfort food); such literal symbols could indicate more conscious than unconscious involvement. This is something that you will get an instinct for the more you use this pattern. You *can* work with a consciously constructed symbol, but the more you can engage the unconscious mind early on, the easier this pattern becomes. If you believe the client does have a consciously constructed symbol, then you may wish to ask about details of the symbol, so that their trance deepens, and the client's unconscious mind becomes more involved.

If the client's symbols are not directly related to the issue on a logical level then you most likely have unconscious involvement. The client may also express her surprise and curiosity at the type of symbols her unconscious mind has presented. For example, in the case of the overweight client, instead of symbols of her skinny and eating, she may generate a symbol of say sunshine in one hand and a rock in the other. Logically, these images have very little to do with the conflicting parts, but at the level of metaphor, they may be extremely significant for the client. Remember the realm of metaphor is also the realm of the unconscious, where the conflicting parts and the conflict itself reside.

When you have elicited the symbols successfully, the unconscious has begun the process of engaging both parts so that change can take place. So the interaction may look something like this:

Coach: Take a moment to imagine what it would be like if you had a symbol to represent this part of you.

Client: All right.

Coach: As you consider that, I'm curious what symbol comes to mind for you that represents this part? [Coach lightly touches the palm of the client's hand.]

Client: That's interesting.

Coach: What is that symbol?

Client: A key.

Coach: That's right, a key.

In this example, the coach starts by suggesting that the client imagine what it would be like if a symbol was to appear. This puts no pressure consciously on the client to come up with a symbol; they can simply daydream about what would happen if one appeared. Meanwhile the unconscious mind hears the level beneath the obvious conscious communication and takes the suggestion to create the symbol onboard. It begins to formulate that symbol without the conscious mind knowing that it is doing so.

As coaches, we like to emphasize a sense of curiosity; curiosity about the client, about their model of the world, the ways in which their problem appears, and the ways in which they're able to resolve it. In the next part of the example the coach expresses that curiosity. This does a couple of things. First, it lets the client step out from underneath the problem. How can you feel bad when you are feeling curious? Curiosity is an unconscious experience, so by accessing it, you are reinforcing the unconscious commitment to create change. Second, this statement about curiosity layers in the presupposition that there *will* be a symbol. This takes away the option for failure. At each step of the process of change, we want to give the client every opportunity to succeed. This reinforces the pattern of yeses, creating an "agreement set" because the client is constantly saying yes to you in indirect ways. This sets a pattern of success in the client's unconscious mind and it means that when the moment of change occurs, they have already agreed to it. Having succeeded in each step of the pattern, the client is ready to take the last small step and successfully resolve the conflict between their parts.

In the above example, eliciting the symbol goes smoothly. Of course there will be certain times, with certain clients, when this step will require more refinement and a little more work on your part as the coach. One common difficulty is the client's inability to see any symbol. Remember: visualization is something that we do automatically, but the ability to recognize it is a skill. So a more challenging interaction may unfold as follows:

Coach: Now, I'm curious what represents this part of you:

what symbol comes to mind?

Client: Nothing

Coach: That's right, nothing yet. And as you carefully consider this part of you, what does come to mind? What are you seeing?

Client: Still nothing . . . I don't see anything

In the above scenario, the client is not recognizing what the unconscious mind is doing. Our minds cannot help but make images; a large portion of our brain is dedicated to visual processing. Creating images is an important part of our neurological functioning. If the coach were to further explore this issue with the client, it would likely have come out that the client believes that visualization is not something that she can "do." The client may feel that she does not have a good imagination, or she could be having an experience that does not match her expectations. There are many ways to get around these issues, and we will suggest a couple here.

First we will tackle the most common difficulty: the client's belief that she cannot visualize or imagine. One of the easiest ways to step around this is to have her think about something very familiar. Here's an example:

Coach: That's right, you really do not think that you can visualize. I would like for you, if you would, to just think about your front door. Now, I don't know if it's an apartment or if it's a door to a house, but you can remember that familiar door. What color is the door?
Client: Red.

Coach: I would like for you to open the door and notice just how high the lock is. How do you know where the doorknob is on your door? And I would like for you to walk inside your home and notice what is on the left.

Client: A table.

Coach: A table. And what is on your right?

Client: A shoe rack.

Coach: Now I would like for you to walk into your living room. What color is your couch?

Client: It is black.

Coach: Go and turn on your TV. What is on TV?

Client: The local news.

Coach: How do you know?

Client: I see it.

Coach: That's right, you see it. And just as you can see your front door, height of the lock, the table to your left, shoe rack on the right, the black couch in your living room, and the local news on your TV, you can use the same part of your mind to create images and symbols because you do it all the time, naturally and easily. It is this part of your mind that can help you now to create new symbols so that you can change and grow as a person.

This is how you can use the client's everyday experiences to show them that they are already making images and symbols in their mind. This process moves an unconscious behavior into the client's conscious awareness so that they can recognize their ability. Once they have this realization, their beliefs around their ability to visualize will change. You can then return to the Visual Squash and elicit the symbols for each part.

One of the other blocks you may encounter around visualization is that the client has certain expectations about what it is he is supposed to see. This issue has two levels: a quality issue and a content issue. In terms of quality, some clients may have the expectation that they should see the symbol as clearly as they see an object in the external world, and while there are some very deep trance subjects who do have this unique ability, most of us notice a lot of difference between imagined and real objects. The client could very well have the symbol in mind as he is looking at his hand, but because his expectation of what he should be seeing does not match what he actually experiences, he blocks the experience. The client will undergo cognitive dissonance, when reality and expectation do not meet and so he is unable to recognize the symbol his unconscious mind has presented because he is expecting something more clear, tangible, and solid.

The second issue, that of content, occurs because the client has a conscious expectation of what the symbol should be. For example, the client discovers the symbol is a boat when she is expecting to see a skinnier version of herself (as in the case of our weight-loss client). Because the content provided by her unconscious does not match her expectation, her conscious mind outright rejects it. The symbol is not "good enough" for her conscious mind. Yet any symbol that the unconscious mind chooses to bring forward is the perfect symbol, and she would be better feeling the freedom to explore her own creative unconscious without conscious limitations and expectations. The fact that the symbol does not match her conscious expectation is in fact a wonderful sign that you're moving in the right direction in the process.

So how do you recognize when there may be a block occurring because of expectations around quality and content? Quite simply the client will tell you, either directly or indirectly. Here's an example, in which the client has already established that he is aware of his ability to visualize:

Coach: And what symbol represents this part of you?

Client: I still don't see anything.

Coach: What is it you are experiencing?

Client: Nothing.

Coach: That's right, you are not experiencing anything yet. If you were to, though, even if you're only imagining it, what would you be experiencing with that part, in that hand right now?
Client: Well, I have a sense of something but I don't really see it.
Coach: And that's fine, you don't have to see it now. And what is it you are sensing in that part?

Client: It is like a boat but I do not see it clearly.

Coach: A boat. And there is nothing you need to be experiencing more than what you are right now, because your unconscious mind is working in just the right way at this moment. What you are experiencing now is exactly what you need to be experiencing to create this change.

In the above example the client has an issue with the quality of the symbol that emerges. It is quite easy to work around this as long as you have rapport with the client. You can suggest that the experience the unconscious mind is creating is just the right one for that moment. Remember, her unconscious mind is tracking both your verbal and nonverbal communication, so be congruent when suggesting this. You need to believe that her unconscious is responding in a way that suits her needs, whether or not she recognizes it consciously. As long as the conscious mind is willing to play with whatever experience may occur, then you are in the right position to proceed. You can even layer in temporal language to suggest that things will become clearer; throughout the examples in this book you will notice the coach using *yet* and *now* to pace the client's current experience, while offering the indirect suggestion that things are changing and her experience will not stay the same.

One final note about clients who report nothing, or that the symbol is blank: that blankness or nothingness could also actually be the symbol the unconscious mind has chosen. To move forward with this, you could give the client a line like this one:

Coach: It's wonderful that you are seeing that nothing. Some clients will see objects or people but you are doing something unique and creative. Your unconscious mind is incredibly creative to develop that symbol through nothingness. If it can do that, I wonder in what other ways your unconscious can use that creativity to help resolve the issue.

In the example below we'll see what happens when the client is having difficulty with the content of the symbol that emerges:

Coach: And what symbol represents that part of you?

Client: I don't know. I want to say a star, but that doesn't make sense. That is not right.

Coach: I'm curious, what makes you think that a star isn't right?

Client: Because it doesn't make any sense. I don't see what it has to do with my problem.

Coach: You're absolutely right, it seems like it has nothing to do with the problem.

Client: What do you mean?

Coach: Logically I know it doesn't make any sense at all that the star should appear to represent that part of you. For whatever reason your unconscious mind has chosen that for you. Would it be OK with you, even though it makes no sense at all, to continue using that star? Think of it as a type of experiment, an experience of just how symbolic your unconscious mind can be in relationship to this problem, and still create that change for you. You don't even have to know consciously what it all means. You can simply enjoy the process. Will that be all right with you?

Client: Yes.

Here we have a client who is not comfortable with the fact that the symbol is something different from what she expected to see. To work through this, first pace the client by acknowledging her experience. You can agree with the client that the symbol does not make sense consciously. As well as helping build rapport, this relieves any pressure on the client, and so helps to bypass any conscious interference. Then you can lead the client away from the idea of logical sense by asking her permission to play with the symbols, suggesting it may be useful and enjoyable to work with them anyway. Asking permission creates another level of "buy-in" for the client. She is agreeing to engage with the process.

So far, you have the client first identifying the different parts of her problem, then associating those parts with either the right or left hand, followed by assigning symbols to those parts. Symbols serve as metaphors. Think of them as bridges that the unconscious mind uses to create meaning and move information between the conscious and unconscious minds. You have now set the scene for the magic to take place! In the next chapter we will explore the use of catalepsy, which is not only a key part of the Visual Squash, but also a useful metaphor for creating change and engaging unconscious processes on a deep level.

Receive your book bonus at www.visualsquashbookbonus.com

Chapter Five: Catalepsy

Catalepsy is a natural state where the unconscious mind takes control of the body, or a body part, and holds it in place with minimal effort. Some describe it as a waxy flexibility. You can experience catalepsy in your whole body, or in individual body parts like an arm or the eye lids. You can imagine, for example, how it would feel if every muscle in your arm were perfectly balanced at the same time, so no single muscle is taking on the entirety of the work of your arm. No muscle is controlling movement in one direction or another.

Catalepsy is an essential feature of the Classic Visual Squash as it allows the coach to track the client's unconscious progress, and also because catalepsy and the unconscious hand movements that develop from it serve as a wonderful "convincer" for the client, showing them that something out of the ordinary is taking place. Just as the symbols for the parts are visual metaphors, catalepsy and the proceeding parts assignment are kinesthetic metaphors for the conflict as well as the change process.

So from the moment you lift the client's hands until the testing phase of this pattern, the client's level of catalepsy indicates where he is in each step of the process. Often, the strangeness of seeing and feeling his hands rise without conscious volition convinces him that his unconscious mind has the power to resolve the conflict. In noticing the strangeness of the catalepsy, he recognizes the difference between this and his day-to-day experience, which means he can more readily believe that a long-standing internal conflict has been resolved.

Catalepsy is a great way of interacting with the

unconscious mind. The body, in many ways, is an extension of unconscious processes. Your heartbeat, breathing, and blink reflex are all regulated by the unconscious. Even the simple act of walking, which requires the coordination of many muscles, sinews, and nerves, is unconscious. If you were to consider each tiny movement that each muscle had to take in order for us to walk while maintaining our balance, we would find it impossible to track consciously.

Because it is unconsciously controlled, the body gives honest responses. In other words, the body expresses emotions and states without being constrained by social expectations. For example a client might think it is inappropriate to verbally acknowledge a feeling and yet their body shows that emotion through the client's breathing, muscle tension, heart rate, and skin tone. The unconscious also moves far quicker than the conscious mind does, and its responses to suggestions and questions can manifest in the body long before there is conscious recognition of what is happening. Catalepsy, and the subsequent unconscious movements and ideomotor responses (micro-muscular movements and twitches) that occur during the Visual Squash, set the pace at which both the coach and client proceed. If there is any part of the experience that is not yet complete, or is out of place, it will be indicated unconsciously perhaps through lack of movement (when movement is expected) or even a movement in the opposite-from-expected direction — for example, hands moving apart instead of closer together. Although the client may think consciously that they're in the right place to continue, the unconscious mind will respond differently through unconscious movements and catalepsy.

Catalepsy might seem intimidating if you are not used to working with it. When someone first witnesses a person in a cataleptic trance, it can be quite an impressive thing. But remember that catalepsy is something that you, your client, and every one of us does naturally and frequently. Have you ever had the experience of standing in a bar or café with some friends, engrossed in an interesting conversation, while holding a glass of wine or cup of coffee? You could be standing there for quite some time but even though you are not aware of the effort of holding it, your glass does not move. You do not drop it. You are holding it cataleptically. Or have you been lost in thought while holding your pen? These are natural occurrences of catalepsy, when your arm is comfortably still as you lose conscious awareness of it. And because we naturally slip in and out of trances at various points in our day, it is easy to elicit catalepsy while working with a client. At one level this will be a novel event for the client, but unconsciously it will be a familiar experience for them, and at the very beginning of this pattern they may not even realize that something unusual is taking place.

One interesting thing about catalepsy is that while it can happen with the client already in trance, it can also induce trance very quickly. It becomes a cataleptic chicken-or-egg question: is the client in trance and catalepsy happens, or does the catalepsy very quickly induce a trance? Once you have induced catalepsy in your client, you do have some level of trance whether or not the client is aware of it, and this is a valuable tool to have because it creates a covert trance. Catalepsy appears again and again in various ways in traditional and Ericksonian hypnotic interactions, NLP coaching sessions, as well as during the client's naturally occurring daily routines. Being able to identify and utilize it will dramatically increase the level of unconscious rapport you have with the client.

If you'd like to experience catalepsy, try this experiment. Sit with your feet on the floor and your hands resting on your lap. Now choose either the left hand or the right hand to be your trance hand for this experiment. Next, begin to lift that hand as slowly as absolutely possible for you. Imagine how it feels for that hand to be moving up millimeter by millimeter. It's as if the hand isn't moving at all. As you do this, begin to notice the quality of the movement in the hand, become aware of the feelings in that hand. You may begin to notice that it doesn't feel like you are lifting it at all anymore, and yet it is still moving. Take your time and allow your body to relax. You can be comfortably curious about what is taking place. When you have finished enjoying this experiment, raise your other hand and take hold of the wrist of the catalectic arm and gently shake it, allowing the muscles to relax as complete and full movement returns to your arm.

As you can see — or, rather, feel — catalepsy is a familiar experience on one level, and yet on another it is completely novel. In fact, your client may not notice their hands are in catalepsy until much later in the process. When you begin utilizing ideomotor movement, they will recognize that something unusual is taking place, but until then, the experience will be normal for them. Of course this also depends on the level of trance that you have induced in your client. If you're working in an uptime trance, using this pattern in a more NLP coaching context, then the catalepsy will probably feel like a normal, common experience between two people having an interesting conversation. If the client is in a deeper trance then you can use the unusual nature of hypnotic catalepsy in ways that compound the positive effects of the pattern. This is how catalepsy can be an induction, a convincer, and a metaphor for change.

In the Visual Squash, when you raise the client's hands and ask them to assign parts to each of them, you are beginning the process of inducing catalepsy, and through catalepsy, trance. It is good practice to ask the client both consciously and unconsciously if it is OK for you to touch their hands and arms during this process. You ask consciously through your words, waiting for a verbal response, either yes or no. You ask unconsciously by touching their hands as you ask. You then watch for their nonverbal response. They may consciously say yes, but if they are not comfortable you will notice an immediate response as you touch their hands. You should always look for both conscious and unconscious agreement. If they consciously say yes and unconsciously say no, you need to do something different. In other words, you should never break unconscious rapport.

The Process

In this section we highlight some of the ways you can both verbally and nonverbally, directly and indirectly, establish catalepsy. Catalepsy is easy for your client to accomplish as long as you expect it to happen and treat it as the natural phenomenon it is. There is no need to even draw your client's attention to their cataleptic arms. As far as they are concerned, the two of you are just having a conversation. It will not be until later, when the hands begin moving together, that it becomes valuable to point out that something unusual is happening. Remember, as we continue on, that anything your client does is exactly right and you can utilize it.

Nonverbal Ways to Establish Catalepsy

The first and easiest way of nonverbally establishing catalepsy is to lift your client's arms in order to assign the parts and then gently move their hands in slightly confusing and unexpected ways. You might lift the client's right hand and assign the part, and as you are doing that you're explaining a little bit about the process.

You gently move their hand up and down and to either side, or gently push up on the back of their hand with your fingers. You will notice a waxy stiffening of the arm and the arm will begin to support itself. You can move both of the client's arms at once, or one at a time; either way, you will begin to notice the client's unconscious mind taking control of the limbs.

One other possibility is utilizing something we call *ambiguous touch*. This means that you gently and randomly touch different parts of the client's arm and hand. This confuses the conscious mind, leaving it not sure exactly where, when, or indeed why you are touching their hand and arm. As a tip, generally, if you lightly touch the back of the arm just above the elbow it tends to activate those muscles responsible for controlling arm movement, thus taking control of the arm. What we are doing is confusing the conscious mind: it is not sure if you are supporting the arm, or if they are expected to support it themselves, so eventually the unconscious mind takes over responsibility for the arm (which of course is what we want). For the client, the arm will feel weightless like it is neither being supported nor held up.

Hypnotic Shelf Metaphor for Creating Catalepsy

There are also verbal tricks that you can use to induce catalepsy in your client. One of them is the metaphor of the *hypnotic shelf*. This allows the client to choose just the right height for their arms in order to create a change. The hypnotic shelf technique goes as follows:

Coach: Now I would like you to imagine that there is a shelf somewhere in front of you. It is an invisible hypnotic shelf that can easily support your arm comfortably. You can just enjoy resting your arm on the shelf. You know what it's like when you're leaning up against something, caught up conversation with someone, while your arm may be resting on a table or on some other surface and you don't even notice; it's just there while you are attending to more important things.

Now you watch as the client's arm drifts, finding just the right level. You may want to support their arm until they find that level, moving it up and down for them. Once they find that shelf, the arm's weight will be supported by the client's unconscious, because their unconscious is responsible for providing the shelf!

This is a nice way of suggesting that the unconscious take responsibility and also that the client need not pay too much conscious attention to the experience of their arm.

The Floating Bird Metaphor for Creating Catalepsy

Another metaphor that we like to use is that of birds. Think about seagulls, for example. When they fly, they very rarely actually flap their wings. Instead they just gently glide, with very little effort needed. It's like resting on a current of air as it moves across the sky. So a coach may say to the client:

Coach: Have you ever seen a bird fly? At first when it takes off it flaps its wings to get to the right height, but then something changes and it simply glides. It allows the air to support it. The difference in air pressure on top of the wing and underneath the wing allows it to glide. It is like the bird is simply resting in midair. I wonder what it would be like for that arm there to experience flying, gliding like a bird, resting on that shelf of air. Effortlessly, comfortably, floating there. That's right!

The goal here is not to give you a script to follow when working with clients but to help you generate new ideas, new metaphors that you can use to describe this experience and elicit it from your clients. There are countless other possibilities.

Training Your Client for Catalepsy

If you have been working with the client hypnotically for a period of time, or if you plan to continue the coaching relationship with them after the Visual Squash, it is useful to teach their unconscious mind how to produce catalepsy automatically. Milton Erickson would hypnotically train all his clients.

You can do this through a number of different kinds of hypnotic experiences most of which are beyond the scope of this book. But to put it concisely, the more often your client experiences any particular trance phenomenon, the easier it is for them to access it in the future. This is the principle of fractionation. The more frequently a hypnotic experience, such as catalepsy, occurs the more skilled the subject becomes at having it. When it is time to do the Visual Squash, you can simply remind them of these previous trances in which they experienced catalepsy by lifting up their arm. This will cause a revivification of the previous trances, so that the arm will naturally develop catalepsy, and the client will go into trance.

How *Not* to Induce Catalepsy

The one thing we suggest you do *not* do to establish catalepsy, particularly with naïve clients (clients who are new or have very little experience in formal hypnosis), is to directly suggest it. This is because the client will then produce it consciously, in which case it's no longer catalepsy and you will not get the same level of unconscious and nonverbal responses as you would like. Also, you run the risk of the client's arm getting tired halfway through the session. If they drop it, it will interrupt the pattern. When an arm is resting in catalepsy, it will not experience the same levels of fatigue as a consciously supported arm, because in catalepsy, all the muscle groups are working together and are equally balanced. That is not to say that the arm won't get tired; it can. But during the process, using genuine catalepsy, the client should not notice.

Troubleshooting Catalepsy

What do you do when a client drops her arms or does not achieve catalepsy? There are many ways of addressing these issues. We will begin with the client who has difficulty experiencing catalepsy. You will recognize this because when you lift their arms to assign the different parts to each hand, they may immediately put them back down. This shows a level of conscious interference. They do not know consciously what is expected of them so they bring the arms back down. Perhaps the arms are heavy and tired, or there is some self-consciousness, or the the client is so consciously confused by not knowing what they should do that they default to what they think is a more socially acceptable position.

The first way of addressing this is to bring their unconscious mind more onboard with the interaction. You can use your language skills, your own state, and your rapport with the client's conscious and unconscious to do this. You can tease the client's unconscious mind until it is participating more and more with the experience. Perhaps you can wonder aloud: "I wonder when your conscious mind will begin to trust your unconscious enough to allow that hand to float comfortably in the air all by itself?" (Notice the various embedded hypnotic commands!) Alternatively, you can simply go back to the nonverbal ways of establishing catalepsy that we talked about at the beginning of the chapter. You can lift the arm and use random movement or ambiguous touch to confuse the conscious mind while nonverbally suggesting to the unconscious mind: it's time to take over.

If, after having done all this, you still have difficulty getting catalepsy, then take a break from this pattern and guide them through the exercise we outlined in the very beginning of this chapter, the one that involves placing your hands on your lap and lifting one of them as slowly as possible, paying attention to all of the different nerves and muscles working to move that hand. It is as if that hand can only lift a millimeter at a time. As they're doing this they will drop into a light trance, at which point you can begin to layer in suggestions about the ease with which they can have this experience, as well as instruct them to remember it at the unconscious level so that they can access it at other times. You may want to be indirect in your communication, to minimize the level of conscious interference in the process. You might say:

Coach: I wonder just how easily you will find that hand slowly rising, almost as if that hand has a mind of its own, and it's good to remember this experience on a deeper level because when that hand is able to lift by itself, and that hand is able to float comfortably in the air, the next time you have this experience, it can be deeper and more profound, as well as more comfortable.

So we have:

"I wonder," a language softener.

"You will find that hand slowly rising," an embedded command.

"That hand" and "mind of its own," dissociation.

"Good to remember," an embedded command.

"Deeper level," a trance suggestion.

"Because," a cause-and-effect pattern.

"That hand is able to lift by itself," an embedded command.

"That time is able to float comfortably," an embedded command and trance suggestion.

"The next time you have this experience," presupposing future catalepsy.

"It can be deeper and more profound, as well as more comfortable," a posthypnotic suggestion and trance suggestion.

You will be able to layer in a lot of suggestions of the above types because your client will be consciously focusing on the movements of their hand rather than paying attention to exactly what you're saying. This distraction makes the suggestions extremely powerful and effective.

From time to time, you may have a client who produces catalepsy long enough to assign the parts, but further along the process they drop their arms. This may be because their conscious mind has become aware of what's happening with those arms; clients will often say that the arms are getting tired when this happens, indicating that there has been a shift from catalepsy to conscious control. Remember, no matter what response your client gives you, it is the right response. If in your mind there is no possible way for your client to fail, then guess what? There is no possible way for your client to fail! Don't make a big deal out of this turn of events: it's something that happens and it's perfectly fine. You may want to even reassure the client that they're still doing the right thing and that they are exactly where they should be in the process. Then, try do something different. This is the beauty of NLP: if something doesn't work, you can always do something different. You can continue on with another form of the Squash, as presented later in this book, or maybe you can take a different approach such as using a Six Step Reframe.

Creating catalepsy is a skill that you will master in a very short time. The more you practice it, the easier it becomes, and the more able you are to develop a sixth sense for when it is working. Have fun with it and experiment with using different patterns in a variety of contexts. Catalepsy is the cornerstone of the Visual Squash; the experience of the hands is a metaphor for the change that is taking place at a deeper level. The body becomes a direct link to the unconscious mind. Mastering catalepsy will prove useful not only in this pattern but in a number of others as well. Using catalepsy, you can even do the Visual Squash completely content-free, relying entirely on catalepsy as an unconscious phenomenon. We will explore this later.

Although we've treated catalepsy as a separate chapter within this book, it's something that you initiate from the start of the Visual Squash. When you assign the different parts to the different hands you can do both hands at the same time or one hand at a time. Which one you choose depends on how experienced your client is with catalepsy. Remember, you can induce catalepsy verbally, through metaphor; nonverbally, by the lifting the arms with random movements; or through ambiguous touch, by very gently and lightly touching different parts the arm.

Having induced catalepsy in your client, you're now ready to move on to the next portion of the pattern: chunking up!

Receive your free catalepsy video at www.visualsquashbonus.com

Chapter Six: Chunking Up

By this point in the process, your client will be experiencing catalepsy in both arms and holding the symbol of each part of the conflict in the palm of each hand. It's time to begin the process of *chunking up*. In this context, chunking up means that you will guide your client to move from the specific issues that she has presented to you and identify the bigger "chunks," or values, that are behind those issues. By values we mean a word that triggers a positive emotion. Of course, different people have different values but words like "love" and "freedom" tend to be common, highly regarded values that make most people feel good. Remember that earlier we discussed the idea that every behavior that the unconscious mind engages in is motivated by a positive intention. The behavior itself may not be agreeable but the motivation behind it is to achieve something good for the client. If the client were not receiving some sort of benefit from the behavior, they would not maintain it. Well, that positive intent is often expressed as a value.

In an extreme example, a murderer may kill to "protect" himself from a perceived threat, or because he thinks he will get something good out of it. Those desires for protection or gain are positive values, although the behavior used to try to achieve them is most definitely not positive! A more realistic example from the field of change work is a client who comes in with a phobia: the phobic reaction is not useful in the outside world, yet for the client's unconscious it is a path to protection and safety, and even beyond that perhaps something greater, like the happiness that comes from feeling safe.

So now it's time to uncover the biggest chunks — the highest possible positive intention — of each part. As you go through this process with your client, and they reach the highest possible intention on each part, keep in mind that the intention should be the same or similar on both sides of tFhe conflict. Both parts of the person need to recognize that they are working on the same team, for the same outcome. They both want to achieve the same goal for the benefit of the person, and once the client recognizes this, the conflict vanishes, and each part can begin to use the abilities of the other part to create a change that will allow them to meet the highest intention in a new and resourceful way.

The question is, what is it we are looking and listening for when talking about the highest positive intention? First, the positive intention should be a nominalization. Nominalizations are a feature of NLP Meta Model language patterns. In linguistics, a nominalization is the use of a verb, an adjective, or an adverb as the head, or most important word, in a noun phrase. Nominalization can also refer specifically to the process of producing a noun from another part of speech. For example, the verb "to transform" can be turned into a noun: transformation. Words like, *happiness, love,* and *freedom* fall into this category.

While we are listening for the nominalization, we are also looking for a key sign that the positive intention has been reached. This sign is a shift in the client into a more positive state; you will see the client light up when the positive intention is found. This state provides the energy necessary for the reintegration to take place. If there is no positive state arising from the positive intention, then the Squash may not work as planned. If the positive energy is there, it will be successful. Think of the state as being both the destination as well as the map: once the person recognizes that both sides have the same state at heart, then the unconscious mind is free to generate new ways of achieving that intention.

When we say that both sides want the same thing, this does not necessarily mean that the description of the positive intent from each side will be the identical. The client may use different words to describe the state. We are primarily looking for congruence in what the client is saying and the state they are experiencing, and descriptions of each positive intention that are mutually supportive and aligned.

Another aspect of the highest positive intention is the idea of *end state energy* (ESE). End state energy describes who or how the person will be once they have this transformation. ESE is not necessarily the same as the client's stated goal — for example, the smoker who wants to quit may state that their goal is to be a nonsmoker, but when chunking up to find the highest positive intention behind the smoking, it may be that the person wants freedom or some other ESE. Another example could be someone who wants more energy, to be more active. However, the ESE may be that they want to have balance in their life. It would not be fitting that for the rest of their life, they walk around every single day with high levels of energy and activity; it's just not appropriate because they would be exhausted! With the ESE, we are looking at the level of identity, because ESE also acts as a type of ecology check: how will the client be different, and how will they sustain this state after they realize their goal? The highest positive intention will give you the ESE for the resolution of the conflict. In this chapter we highlight exactly how to speak to the client to uncover the highest positive intention, nominalization, and end state energy.

To begin the process of chunking up, we first need to explore exactly what a chunk is. A *chunk* is quite simply the way, or the size, in which we view information. We can have large chunks or small chunks and we can chunk up and down. Large chunks are big pieces of information, for example, a view of the entire system. Suppose a client comes in for help with anxiety and the coach asks when and where specifically they feel this anxiety and the client's response is "All the time" or "Always." This is an example of a very large chunk, meaning, they generalize across time and see the world in absolutes. The coach then has the task of chunking down into much smaller pieces of information. For the client with anxiety, that would be moving them from a place where they see themselves as having this issue all the time to a place where they can recognize that in fact they only experience the issue at specific times and specific places. Chunking down ultimately takes a nominalization (anxiety) and turns it back into a verb; the client doesn't have anxiety, they are simply feeling anxious at certain times. In this example, the coach could possibly get a shift in the client by gently teasing them first by asking if they're feeling anxious during the session, or by asking them in a lighthearted way if they feel anxious when they're in the shower, or when they're asleep. Asking questions like this directs the client's attention to smaller, more specific chunks of information ("when I'm asleep" versus "always"). This results in showing the client that the problem is not as big as they originally thought, making a distinction between behavior and identity, and providing a specific issue to work with (specific as to time and place).

According to the NLP idea of Logical Levels, we experience the world through environment, behaviors, capabilities, beliefs, values, and identity. A client may come in with a particular issue he has chunked up to such a large scale that he takes on the issue or problem as his identity. For example, "I am a smoker," "I am an anxious person," or "I am depressed"; all of these are identities the client will take on for himself. We begin to chunk the client down from the larger conception of the problem to something far more manageable; from the level of identity ("I am"), down to the level of state ("I feel" or "I was feeling") and behavior ("I do" or "I did"). The client no longer experiences himself as "being" that specific issue that he wants to work through, but instead he can be just himself even though at that time he is experiencing a state or behavior that is not particularly resourceful.

Working on the level of identity can prove to be far more difficult and challenging than working at the levels of state and behavior. We are interested in the levels of state and behavior much more so than the level of identity because states are easily accessible, so it is useful to be able to chunk down in this respect when clients have generalized the problem to the level of identity.

This isn't the case all of the time: when we are working with positives it is useful to move the client up the ladder, to chunk them up to a much larger idea, moving them to a greater concept of who they are. Many times when we are trying to get to the highest positive intention of the particular part, the client will be parsing information in very small chunks. For example, the coach could ask the client "What is this part doing for you?" The client may then respond, "It's making me eat unhealthily," in the case of a weight-loss client. When this happens they have locked the part in at the level of behavior, which for our purposes isn't particularly useful because the behaviors will necessarily be different (either they eat healthily or they eat unhealthily). We are looking for the positive intention above and beyond the behavior, what is driving that behavior, and this is usually a value. We could ask the client why they are doing the behavior, however, the likelihood of them actually knowing consciously is slim. When you ask why, you run the risk of getting a laundry list of conscious after-the-fact justifications: "I smoked because my boss shouted at me." These could range from levels of practicality to emotions, however, it will be very difficult for the client to immediately reach a clear and congruent answer when the information is coming from the conscious mind as opposed to the unconscious mind.

Therefore we begin to chunk the client up one step at a time to continue to stimulate unconscious processes; after a while the conscious mind will run out of justifications and allow the unconscious mind to present positive intentions. This process may take a little bit of time but the entirety of this pattern is not very long. With the right kind of coaching the client will reach the highest positive intention for each part quite quickly. You will know you've reached the highest positive intention when both parts of them give the same, or very similar, response, including the state change.

Discovering the Shared Positive Intention Above Each Side

Once you have the symbol for each part, you begin chunking up. We suggest beginning with the more positive part, which is usually whatever the goal is. In the case of a toward-toward issue, where both sides appear to be positive from the start, begin with the part that desires the change, or that seems to carry the most energy. This is for one key reason: it's easier! Think about it this way: the negative part, or the part that is holding the client back, will be viewed at some level as being bad or unwanted, not doing anything positive for the person; this makes the process of finding the positive intention for this part far more challenging than it has to be. Even though you may preframe the pattern with an explanation to the client that the idea that every behavior has a positive intention behind it, for some clients this is a very difficult concept to fully accept. They may agree at one level but still have doubts or reservations on another. So when you begin on the positive side you're more likely to get a good response and then when it's time to move to the more negative part, the client's unconscious mind is already primed toward the positive.

Humans sort by state. This means how you're feeling will determine what it is you're seeing in the outside world. There was a study conducted years ago in the UK where a one hundred-pound note was left on the ground. Researchers then tracked how many people picked up the free money and how many simply walked right past it. Afterward they would stop each person who walked by and asked them a few brief questions. There was one question in particular that they were interested in: whether or not the person felt they were lucky in life. What the study showed was that the vast majority of people who picked up the note felt lucky in various parts of their life, while those who did not pick up the note reported both not seeing it on the ground as well as not feeling that they were particularly lucky in life. This shows that our internal state and our frame of mind shape our reality and our experiences of, and interactions with, the outside world.

The process of chunking will take all your finesse and skill because the way you are asking our client to think about their problem is not ordinary for them. It is not a way they are used to considering both the resource and the problem. You are guiding them to the level of value or even identity. You are also moving the client into what John Overdurf, the creator of HNLP and attention shifting coaching, calls "the Void." This is a space in the client's mind that is free from the mental loops they normally run in their heads. Think of this as a moment of complete conscious confusion during which they're able to unconsciously access new information inside of themselves.

To begin the process of chunking up there are many different ways you can ask the client to consider her goal or problem. The easiest way to do this is to ask directly "what this side wants for you," or one of the other questions listed below. This gives you the opening to begin moving up the chunk ladder. Now, of course this will be a slightly different process when you begin working with the problem state. That will be addressed a little bit farther along. For now, staying with the resource state, begin to invite the client to consider the precise things that that side of her is doing for her or wants for her.

Some examples of chunking questions:

What does this side want for you? (Positive intention)

What is this side doing for you? (Behavior)

When you have that, what else do you have? (Result)

When you have this, how will you feel? (State)

Why is that important? (Value)

When you have this, who will you be that is different from now? (Identity)

The client usually has an easy time listing all of the positive things that side is doing for them or wants for them. You may find yourself with a whole list of nominalizations. Remember, it is not simply the nominalization you're looking for; the key to being certain you have reached a high enough chunk is in the *synesthesia*, meaning, you are looking for a positive emotional reaction to the nominalization they give. Their BMIRs (Behavioral Manifestations of Internal Representations) and their physiology, will light up when you have reached a high enough chunk. As you practice this, your sense for determining the right size chunk will become more refined. Don't forget that if the emotional energy is not there, you have not reached a high enough chunk, or you have gone too far and forced the client to think more cognitively, resulting in them losing the emotional connection to the positive intention.

Sometimes clients will find a lower-level chunk and loop around that. What this means is that there will be little to no emotional charge behind the nominalization they provide, and as you continue to ask them they will continue to give you the same word or very similar responses. For example:

Coach: And what does that side want for you?

Client: It wants me to be safe.

Coach: When you are safe, how do you feel?

Client: Secure.

Coach: And when you're secure, who are you as a person?

Client: Protected.

Coach: And when you're protected, who are you as a person?

Client: Safe.

A simple way of addressing this is to list each nominalization the client has provided, which will make them feel obliged to at least come up with new material!

Coach: And when you're safe, secure, and protected, who will you be as a person?

STEM Predicates

In the example above, the client is cycling around the same ideas, even without the repetition of the word *safe*. An easy way to move them out of that loop is to begin using specific types of predicates that move awareness from where it was to somewhere it has not yet been. In grammar, a predicate is a word or phrase that modifies the subject of a sentence. In NLP, we use STEM predicates to modify how a client is thinking about their problem. STEM is an acronym — it stands for Space, Time, Energy, Matter. Each of these categories represents a group of words and questions we can use to help shift the client's thinking. This is sometimes called *Mind Bending Language* (Igor Ledochowski) or *Attention Shifting Language* (John Overdurf). Questions using STEM predicates might not sound a little funny grammatically, but they are very effective at shifting the client's unconscious responses into something you can more easily work with.

If we were to ask you to consider some small problem that you have experienced recently, you could maybe recall an argument, a deadline you didn't meet, or some other small issue where you were not feeling very resourceful. Do you notice where you are? Are you alone or with other people? Do you notice what you're seeing, hearing, and how it feels at that moment? As you get in touch with a little bit of this unresourceful feeling, consider the following questions:

1) What is just on the other side of that problem that can increase a good feeling deep inside?

2) What feelings of comfort can you identify after that situation has been resolved, and just before you realize that you can choose a new way to feel?

3) How quickly can that feeling slow down enough to transform?

4) How powerful is your ability to feel comfort in this situation, and in many others?

The ways in which we use language can have a profound effect on emotional states and thought processes. As you read the questions above, what did you notice in your own state? The language used here is based on the principle that we can shift and direct attention in a way that creates more space in the mind of the client. This is very useful when a client becomes stuck, as in the example above concerning safety. Using STEM predicates can guide you through this redirection. Let's look at the categories in more detail.

Spatial Predicates

The first type of predicate is *spatial prepositions*. These are words that indicate physical location and distancing. Spatial predicates are fascinating because they literally move unconscious awareness from one location to another, without the conscious mind being aware of exactly what is being asked. They also locate problems or thought loops within a "physical" sphere created by the unconscious. The thought loop that the client is stuck in becomes something that has things in front of it, behind it, before it, across from it, and so on. Below, you will find a shortlist of spatial predicates that are quite useful in moving clients along the process of chunking up.

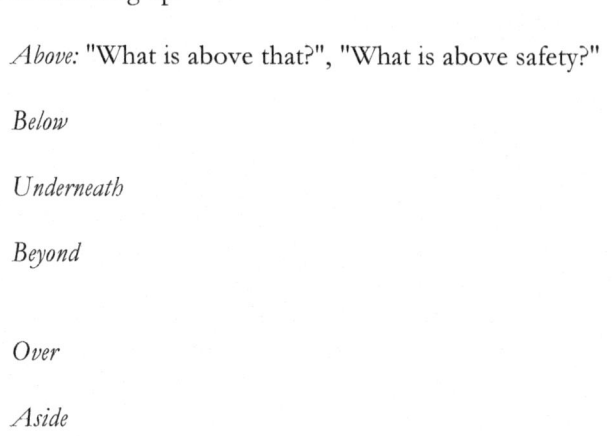

Above: "What is above that?", "What is above safety?"

Below

Underneath

Beyond

Over

Aside

Inside

Outside

Time Predicates

The next set of predicates is *temporal predicates*, or orientations in time. Temporal predicates place the thought loop at a specific point on the client's timeline, which means there will always be things that are before it and come after it. The goal of temporal predicates is to move the client farther along on their timeline. So when a client is caught in a loop, as with the "safe" client above, you can encourage them to consider what happens after they have the safety, security, and protection. This acknowledges that the loop exists in the client's experience but that it does not last the entirety of it, and that there is something that comes after. Because the problem now occupies only a moment of time, it forces the client to acknowledge that, yes, that thought is there and yet there is something else after (and before) it. They will need to move in time to access the information you're asking for.

After: "What happens after you have safety, security, and protection?" "What happens after you feel safe, secure, and protected?"

Before

When

Earlier

Later

Energy Predicates

Energy predicates fall within the category of adverbs, the quality with which something is done. Energy implies movement. This is a way of shifting the client's attention with a particular quality. Energy predicates can be useful when chunking up, however, space and time tend to move the client out of their loop more quickly.

Quickly: "How quickly can you begin to feel that sense of safety grow?"
Slowly

Easily

Energetically

Smoothly

Confidently

Matter Predicates

Finally, *matter predicates* are the ways in which we describe things, for example, nouns (what), quantifiers (how many), and adjectives (what sort). These provide a context or the nature of the problem or conflict. Matter predicates include words related to size, shape, color, and other ways of describing objects in the physical world. These are the predicates we listen for when speaking with clients, to understand their preferred representational system — visual, auditory, kinesthetic, etc.

This

That

Other

Everything

All

Nothing

These

Those

The goal of all of these predicates is to move the client from where they are to a place where they have not yet been. As we previously mentioned, John Overdurf refers to this as the Void. This is a state of mind in which the conscious mind does not have access to its normal mode of functioning. The information and experiences the conscious mind relies on to maintain that particular problem state are not located in the Void. The Void is also an incredibly resourceful place because it is a direct unconscious experience. Every single person has all of the resources they need to make changes to achieve their goals; it is simply a matter of contacting those resources. When the client is in the Void, ties to his normal consciousness have been severed and he is free to explore new possibilities, infinite possibilities. Entering the Void means that he can no longer think in the same way he did before that moment. When using STEM predicates, you will see a direct shift in the client when the thought they were caught in has been broken. They will enter a transderivational search and you will see their eyes search for information, perhaps scanning backward and forward in the space above them, a mini trance.

An Example of Chunking Up

Using the example from the beginning of the book, here is an example of the chunking up process. You will be able to spot the thought loops and use of language that moved the client into a new way of thinking about the parts of their conflict.

Coach: It's giving you a path.

Client: Yeah.

Coach: And when you have that path, how does it feel?

Client: It feels like I know where I'm going.

Coach: And what is that experience like?

Client: It's regular — no, routine.

Coach: And what does that routine give you?

Client: Um I'm spinning….Safety.

Coach: And what do you get from having that safety?

Client: Oh, maybe I can be myself in other areas.

Coach: You can be yourself in other areas. You can be yourself in other areas. This part over here that wants you to discover who you are, what is it doing for you?

Client: Self-actualization.

Coach: And when you're self-actualized?

Client: I'm me.

Coach: And how does that feel?

Client: Good. [Physiological shift]

Coach: Good. And when you've taken the path and realized you can be yourself [points to problem side], how does that feel?

Client: Good. [Physiological shift]

Coach: You mean both sides want you to feel good?

Client: Yeah.

Normally the description of *good* would not be a strong enough chunk because it tends not to hold enough emotional energy; however, in the case of this particular client, the nominalization elicited a strong positive state change, so it was accepted.

Once the positive intention behind the resource has been uncovered, the process can begin for the part that is in conflict. Depending on the client, chunking up on this side can either go quickly or can take slightly longer than the positive side. In the example above, once the positive intention for the resource was discovered, it was very easy to chunk up on the other side. This client's unconscious mind saw the pattern and applied it quickly so that it required far less dancing to reach the same intention on the side of the conflicting part.

One issue that can arise from time to time when working on the more negative side is that despite your pre-frames, the client has a difficult time finding anything positive from that side. When the coach begins to ask what that side is doing for the client, the client may respond by saying, "It's doing nothing for me at all." Or she may respond by saying that it is doing something specific and negative. For example, when doing the Visual Squash with someone who would like to stop smoking, the coach may ask what the smoking side is doing for the client and the client could respond with things like "It's making me sick, taking my money, and making me feel bad." These responses are going in the wrong direction, so we need to guide the client back to the idea that there is something positive to be found. You can do this by first reminding the client that every behavior has a positive intention behind it, even if the behavior is not useful. As long as they accept this pre-frame at the beginning of the session, they will begin the process of moving the mind in the right direction.

Just as when you have someone who becomes stuck in a thought loop, when you have a client stuck in the negative you can use different types of language, such as STEM predicates, presented above, to move their thoughts to a new place. Here is an example, using a client who wants to quite smoking:

Coach: And what is this one doing for you?

Client: Nothing.

Coach: Do you normally do things without any reason behind them?

Client: No.

Coach: That's right, you don't. I wonder what this side wants for you.

Client: It wants to make me cough, feel bad, and get sick.

Coach: And aside from all of these negative things, if you were to imagine this side wants something good for you, what would that be?

Client: To belong.

Once the coach has a foot in the door, the process of chunking becomes very easy and straightforward. In the example above, once the client responded with wanting to belong, then we began to look at what the reasons behind belonging are. In terms of getting the client to that point, as you can see above, the coach used very simple application of a spatial predicate — "aside" — to create small spins in the client's mind. Complex and overly thought-out language patterns aren't necessary. Simply by using predicates in appropriate places, the client's thought processes begin to function differently.

Another way to make this easier is to encourage the client to imagine what it would be like if there was a positive motivation. This is a covert way of sending the client's mind on a search to access the information. If the client is simply imagining it, then they have the freedom to try on positive intentions without being invested in actually consciously accepting the idea that there is a positive behind it. For some clients, imagining positive intentions feels safer, and chunking up becomes an exploration of possibilities. Whether the client is asked to imagine or not, the result is still the same. This is because imagination is an unconscious process and the unconscious mind doesn't distinguish between that which is imagined and that which exists in the outside world.

When chunking up, keep in mind that it is possible to chunk too high. If you move too far into the land of abstractions you could cycle on forever. Throughout this process, you are calibrating the client's state. If there is a decrease in their state, then you may have chunked up too far and will need to move back down a level or two, to where their state was more definitely positive.

Finally, remember that the process of change is a verbal dance. Coach and client are always dancing and the use of patterns is meant to give you flexibility. NLP patterns are not one-size-fits-all, nor are they exact recipes. The more flexible you are, the greater the opportunity for change will be. Your client will be inflexible when doing the specific problem, and it is when you introduce flexibility that they change. The chunking up process is a wonderful opportunity to experience this flexibility, because it really is a self-exploration for the client. In the example at the beginning of the book this was the case; when the coach began chunking up, it became clear that the parts were not accurate, it was not "consulting" and "writing," it was the client wanting to discover who he was, and not wanting to know. Once the right parts were placed in his hands, the client easily found the highest positive intention.

Now that we have a highest shared positive intention, the rest of the reintegration process is straightforward, as we will explain in the next chapter.

Receive your book bonus at www.visualsquashbookbonus.com

Chapter Seven: Reintegration

Once the client has chunked up to the highest positive intention, the steps become much easier because the client is now comfortable with thinking of both parts as positive.

The first step of the final part of the Squash is finding the hidden abilities or skills contained in each part, and sharing those abilities with the other part. This is a powerful reframe for both parts of the conflict because they can begin to help rather than clash with each other. Because we are incredibly resourceful creatures, there are different abilities and skills that we allocate for different aspect of our behavior and states, and each of the parts will have different skills and abilities, one keeping them safe perhaps, while the other looks for opportunity. When the client has accepted that the conflicting or negative part wants something good for them, the reframe of a hidden skill or ability leads them to further accept that part as a part of who they are, not a part to be rejected and pushed away. This reframe works on two levels: the first level allows the client to recognize that part as part of herself so that the rest of the integration happens automatically. On a deeper level, acceptance of the hidden abilities is a sign that the client has taken on board the Visual Squash reframe of reintegration to its fullest extent.

Finding the hidden ability also places both the positive part and the conflicting part under the client's control. Think of it this way: when you have a skill, you have control over it and you get to decide when and where that skill is used. This is the transformation of a problem into a resource, because there may be specific times and places where the conflicting part is not only useful but also valuable. Recognizing this hidden ability allows the integration to take place in an ecological way because the unconscious mind does not need to give up on that part; it simply uses it in a new way. Finding a hidden ability for both parts is also an ecology check, making sure that nothing of value from either part is lost during the reintegration. Both sides have important things that can be offered to the client!

The process for discovering the hidden ability is quite simple: you simply ask the client. Beginning once again with the positive side, have the client consider what type of skills that side can give to them and, more importantly, can give to the conflicting part. Just like in the chunking process, we begin with the positive part because it is easier. Once again your client will give you a number of nominalizations. For example, they may say that that part gives strength, comfort, a sense of self, or other positive abilities and qualities.

Throughout this process the coach both consciously and unconsciously suggests the gifting of these abilities from the positive side to the conflicting part. Consciously this is done through direct suggestion. When asking the client about the abilities, the questions are framed in a way that suggests both the client and the conflicting part could find that skill useful — "And how could this other part find strength useful?"

Unconsciously we suggest the gifting of the ability from one side to the other through touch and gesture. When asking the client about the hidden ability, we lightly touch the hand associated with that ability and then we touch the opposite hand containing the conflicting part, moving from the hand that already has the ability to the hand that doesn't. Throughout this process, and as the client becomes more involved with discerning the skills and abilities contained in each part, you as the coach can continue to unconsciously acknowledge each part in a way that becomes confusing to the conscious mind. For example, after the client begins naming a number of resources, the coach ambiguously touches the each hand in no particular order. This unconsciously suggests that reintegration has already begun. One side giving to the other, the other side giving back, so that it becomes consciously confusing to the client. The client can easily lose track of the nonverbal communication, while the unconscious mind understands the implication with ease.

When working with the positive side of the conflict, it is very rare that the client will not be able to find hidden resources and abilities, and in fact the client will likely generate a number of them. In the case where a client does not, it may simply be an issue of them not completely understanding what you're asking them to do, in which case you can use your language skills and your hypnotic abilities to lead them in the direction of finding those resources.

Once the client has recognized a number of abilities, you can move on to the conflicting side. With some clients, this side will be easy to work with. This is because their unconscious mind has fully understood and taken on board the reframes that you have already given. They have taken the experience from the positive side and at the unconscious level said to themselves, "I understand what to do here."

For others, this part of the process may still be a bit challenging. While they do recognize that there is a positive intention behind that conflicting part, they are not used to seeing that side of themselves as being particularly resourceful. In these cases, it may be useful to begin the process by suggesting a resource that is inherently a part of the problem — for example, persistence. That conflicting part has stayed around no matter how much the client has tried to move around it. Persistence is a wonderful skill for the positive side to take on board. When that positive side is as persistent as the conflicting part had been in the past, then the conflict will resolve itself.

On the rare occasion that the client does not accept the idea that there are skills and resources inherent in the negative part, a piece is missing in the previous steps of the process. You may find that in the elicitation of the highest positive intention that there was not a strong positive state shift for the negative part. It is essential for the client to accept the frames around the Squash for it to be successful. If the client still refuses to acknowledge the positive skills of the conflicting part, you as the coach will need to take a step back and return to the idea of the highest positive attention. When a client recognizes the negative part as having at least one skill — for example, the fact that that problem has stayed with them for so long — they begin to generate other skills.

Physical Reintegration

In Chapter Four, we spoke about catalepsy and the body being an extension of the unconscious mind. Catalepsy becomes a powerful hypnotic metaphor for the changes taking place at the deepest levels of the client's unconscious mind. Now, you may notice something very interesting happen once your client reaches the highest positive intention on both sides. Oftentimes their unconscious mind understands the metaphor of having a part in each hand well before the conscious mind has a chance to realize what is happening. Once the shared highest positive intention on both sides has been discovered, the client's hands may begin to move together on their own. This can happen slowly or sometimes so quickly that you actually have to slow the process in order to chunk up the skills for both sides before the hands meet!

This part of the process is where the client can consciously recognize that there is a change that has taken place. Unconsciously the change happened when they reached the same highest positive intention and recognized the skill sets inherent in both sides. The external symbol, the visual metaphor for this change, can be found in this step, and also the hands coming together and the client being presented with a new symbol. This represents the joining of resources, one side giving its skills and abilities to the other and the other side doing the same. It is also an outward sign that both parts of the conflict do indeed actually want the same thing for the benefit of the client. When the hands do join together the client recognizes both consciously and unconsciously that the process of transformation is taking place.

To help the process of natural reintegration to occur without your direct suggestion, you can begin with unconscious suggestions in the pre-frames that you set. The easiest way to do this is through hand gestures when describing the process. For example, when you are echoing to the client their conflict during the initial phase of reintegration, you can gesture with your own hands. One part is in one hand, the other part in the other, and then you casually bringing your own hands together. This seems like a very unimportant and almost trivial gesture; the client will not consciously recognize it as being of importance. But you are demonstrating to his unconscious what you expect later in the pattern. Consciously you are simply you moving your hands as you're continuing to speak with him about the conflict, however, at the unconscious level you are giving direct suggestions to the deeper parts to start working together. When the time comes in the session for the physical reintegration to take place, the unconscious mind has already been formatted for it.

If the client's hands do not automatically come together, suggest verbally and nonverbally that this process take place. A coach may say to a client:

Coach: So now that you have both parts of you wanting the same thing, and sharing the skills, I think it's time that they start working together. How about you?

Client: Yes, I agree.

As you make the statement, you may again bring your hands together, mirroring what is expected. You may also gently touch the back of each of the client's hands, subtly suggesting that they move inward. We are not forcing the hands to come together; in fact, this would not be useful, as hands coming together are the signal that the unconscious mind has accepted the reframes. The client may consciously recognize this as a suggestion for the hands to move or they may not. If you choose to use ambiguous touch, be very gentle. The importance of this technique is simply to give the suggestion that both parts can physically come together.

Some very interesting things can take place at this point. If the hands come together unconsciously, the client will be pleasantly surprised. It is not uncommon for clients to openly express their amazement. This is a wonderful opportunity for you to give positive suggestions to reinforce the work already done, "That's wonderful, it means this integration is taking place on the deepest unconscious level." The client is in trance, even if they do not recognize it, and they're feeling good and pleased that their hands are moving all on their own. You as the coach have a direct "in" with their unconscious mind. Use this opportunity to continue to build resources for the client.

As the hands begin moving together this is your opportunity to also suggest integration through language. This is done indirectly by the mixing and matching of the client's statements from the chunking up process. Think of this as linguistically weaving together both parts of the client. You may take a resource from the left side and mix it with a resource from the right side. You may remind the client that both sides want the same thing and encourage them to be curious about just how the right side is going to use the left side's resources. Below is an example of this from the client session presented at the beginning of this book.

Coach: So what I would like for you to do is to watch these because they have already begun a journey and eventually, in their own time, when they do touch, I would like for your unconscious mind to create a new symbol. This new symbol lets you know that both parts are working together, because each side of you has something to give the other side. This part of you that will give safety and can let you feel good on that path, it has a skill that it can give this other side to help you discover who you are. What is that skill?

Client: It's like practicality, getting things done.

Coach: Practicality and getting things done. What about this side over here? What skill can it give?

Client: Vision and growth.

Coach: Practicality, getting things done, vision and growth [touches both hands, confusing the sides with the skills]. And as those hands come together, your unconscious mind prepares that new symbol. Vision and practicality, getting things done, and growth. That's right . . . that's it.

The coach is continuously echoing the client's words, as well as the different chunks of information that the client had presented. During the chunking process, although the client does not have a major shift until the highest positive intention is found, the nominalizations they provide throughout the process are still useful and you as coach need to track and remember them. For the client, those lower-level nominalizations still have a connection to or in some way represent each part. So once again you're simply mixing and matching the client's nominalizations, as well as the skill sets that each part brings to the table. This communicates to the unconscious mind that it's time to move all of these pieces together to generate a more powerful resource state for the client. It also reaffirms that those other normalizations are still of value and that those other purposes behind each behavior are still important. As long as they are positive they can be of value to the client.

In the event the hands do not come together, it may be because you have not chunked up to the highest positive intention yet. If so, the process may still work, but the chances of a positive, generative, and lasting change are significantly diminished. This is why we as coaches cannot suggest what that positive intention may be, even if we think we know what it is. The unconscious mind needs to have the reference experiences of that positive intention as it is contained within the conflicting parts, in order to create the integrative experience.

Reintegration also may not work because of an ecology issue: the unconscious mind has decided that it would not be of value for the client to have both parts integrated. For example, it may be that there may be a secondary gain issue hidden within the desire to keep both parts separate. You can do a Visual Squash on the secondary gain issue first before moving specifically onto the client's original conflict. Ecology issues should not factor in too greatly as long as you have done ecology checks throughout the process. If there were going to be a difficulty with ecology issues you would most likely experience it when eliciting the values when you're chunking up.

The easiest way to spot an issue with reintegration is in the movement of the hands. You will notice one of three things; the hands stay completely still where they are, they begin to move away from each other, or the client is consciously moving them. Because the body is an extension of the unconscious mind, both the lack of movement and the movement apart are direct communications that something needs to be changed. Either the client is stuck, the highest positive intention has not been reached, or the right skills for both parts have not been addressed yet. If the hands begin to move apart, this is the unconscious mind saying that it is not ready to integrate these parts yet and there may be a secondary gain issue occurring. In that case, return to the chunking up of the highest positive intention. If after going through the process another time you're getting the same results, you have options. You can either explore this further with your client. Or it may be more useful to take a different approach. If it isn't working, do something different. Everything the client gives you is feedback and neither you as the coach, nor your client, can fail as long as you remain flexible.

This brings us to an important note. In the coaching process we want to give the client as many experiences as possible of succeeding. This acts as a covert agreements set, and it formats the unconscious mind to succeed at the change work. If the client's hands move apart or don't respond even after stepping back and beginning the process again, you can simply frame it as being a success in another way. Just as the client finds hidden skills and abilities within the conflicting parts, so too is there a hidden skill or ability in the lack of movement. You could reframe it in a number of ways depending on the context of the session. The client who wants more confidence could be confidently showing that they can change in the way that makes the most sense, for example.

A client's feeling of success establishes an agreement set. With each success the client is unconsciously saying yes to your process, so it becomes easier and easier for them to continue to agree with you at the unconscious level. And success formats the unconscious mind for more success. The unconscious mind has a strong ability to generalize. We learn very, very quickly because we are able to unconsciously recognize patterns and begin to future pace. Each small success within a session points the mind in the direction of greater success as you continue. Smaller successes are like hypnotic suggestions, getting the mind ready for the larger change about to take place.

If you notice conscious movement, which is far smoother and quicker than unconscious movement, the client may be consciously complying with you while unconsciously, something is off. You can check what is happening by asking the client to slow down, or suggest slowing down by gently restraining the hands from moving together. The conscious mind will take this as a suggestion not to move the hands, perhaps allowing the unconscious mind to take over and continue integration through catalepsy.

On a final note about instances when the hands do not move together, there is one simple step that you can take that many coaches overlook. If you're not seeing the results you expected, you can always ask the client, "What's happening now?" Too many coaches are afraid to ask this. They do not want to imply something is wrong, or that they don't know where they are in the process. This is avoided when you ask with a sense of pure curiosity about the client's experience. The client knows much more about what's happening inside themselves, and their own emotional states than we do. At this point they've been in and out of several different trances, the unconscious mind is closer to the surface and ready to communicate. So feel secure in asking your client what is happening because then you can have a more detailed roadmap of how to get to a more resourceful state.

Eliciting a Transformative Symbol

Once the hands have touched it is time to reorient the client back into their visual experience. The Visual Squash works on three different levels of internal representations: it uses the visual (eliciting symbols), kinesthetic (catalepsy and unconscious movement), and auditory experiences (the chunking up and labeling process). The entire Squash cycles through the client's visual, auditory, and kinesthetic (VAK) representational systems. The final visual symbol is a merging of the two symbols elicited earlier in the process. This new, integrated symbol becomes a resource, a visual anchor for the new state. This also acts as another convincer to the client of the changes that have taken place.

As the hands are moving together, the coach suggests to the client that when they touch, a new symbol will appear representing the change that is taking place, a resolution of the conflict, and the development of even more refined resources. During this process it is useful to chunk up the idea that the symbol will be different, new, that it will not look like a combination of the symbols on the two hands. You guide the client to create a completely new symbol, and therefore a new resource. The appearance of the new symbol is a sign that the unconscious mind has found a new way of meeting its highest positive intention.

It is not uncommon for the new symbol to be somewhat abstract compared to the previous two symbols. It may take the form of light, water, or something else that is nonspecific in terms of shape and size. Some clients will describe a feeling. In these cases the client may very well be visually registering the symbol for that emotion; however, it is more difficult to describe the symbol in terms of physical characteristics than it is in terms of the emotional feeling. All symbols at this point in the reintegration, whether abstract or concrete, should have an emotional charge to them.

This lets the client confirm that things are different, and they have a new mode of approaching the context that was once the conflict.

The process for eliciting the new, fully integrated symbol is slightly modified from the process we use at the beginning of the Visual Squash. At the beginning of the Visual Squash the language is far more open-ended as we invite the client to imagine what it would be like, or what could represent that particular part. Linguistically we give the client a sense of choice, a type of double bind. For example, when we ask the client, "If there is a symbol to represent part A, what would that symbol be," the client has the illusion of choice between there being a symbol which they see, or there not being a symbol, which they can imagine seeing! Of course, the language indirectly suggests that they will see a symbol. The opening for the Squash therefore is far more permissive in laying groundwork for change. Once we get to the point of the reintegration, you as the coach can be far more direct. The client has already experienced either overt or covert trance during this process. They have had arm catalepsy, ideomotor movements, as well as the experience of discovering symbols. At this point the coach can be far more direct that the client will see a new symbol. This takes away any illusion of choice about whether or not the change has actually taken place. Because the client has already been through several cycles of agreement with you as the coach, their unconscious mind is primed to respond with a new symbol.

The phrasing of this is really up to you. You can suggest that as the hands come together the unconscious mind is creating a new symbol. If you recall the session at the beginning of this book, you can find other examples of the wording for this part of the process. Below is an excerpt from that session so you can have a sense of the type of language used to elicit that final symbol.

Coach: So what I would like for you to do is to watch these hands because they have already begun a journey, and eventually, in their own time, when they do touch, I would like for your unconscious mind to create a new symbol. This new symbol lets you know that both parts are working together because each side of you has something to give the other side. This part of you that will give safety and can let you feel good on that path, it has a skill that it can give this other side to help you discover who you are. What is that skill?

Client: It's like practicality, getting things done.

Coach: Practicality and getting things done. What about this side over here? What skill can it give?

Client: Vision and growth.

Coach: Practicality, getting things done, vision, and growth. [Touches both hands, begins to touch the "wrong" side as she mentions each skill.] And as those hands come together, your unconscious mind prepares that new symbol. Vision and practicality, getting things done, and growth. That's right . . . that's it. And when those hands do touch, that symbol will appear in its own time. That's it. What is that there? [Client's hands touch.] What do you see there?

Client: I see a rope going up like the Indian Rope Trick.

Coach: I'd like for you to take that rope going up and make it a part of who you are in any way that is appropriate for you. Practicality, growth, vision, getting things done — that rope going up represents discovering who you are, following a path, having others around you while discovering who you are. Maybe even a routine way of making discoveries.

[Client smiles.]

Coach: Only when that rope is fully integrated, and all parts of you are working together, can you keep feeling good and practically having vision and growth in a way that gets things done. Now, you can your eyes open and return to the room, with full movement in your arms. In your own time.

It is your job to be 100 percent congruent with the message you are giving the client. As in any piece of change work, if you have doubts about the client's ability to have the experience you're suggesting, then those doubts will be subcommunicated to the client's unconscious mind. Therefore, have no doubt that that new symbol will appear. Both you and your client have all the resources both of you need for the client to have this experience.

There will be instances where some clients experience difficulty recognizing this new symbol. Sometimes a client will say that they do not see anything, that there is nothing there. One of two things may be occurring. First, you did not chunk up high enough on the positive intentions (or too high) and/or there is no emotional energy directing the change. In this case it's simply a process of going back and starting again, or starting at the level where there was emotional energy in the nominalizations. The client does not know the pattern; they have no idea what each of the steps are or the order of the steps. You can feel confident that going back to an earlier stage in the process will be fine. Second, it is possible that the "veil of consciousness," otherwise known as the client's critical mind, is preventing the client from seeing the new symbol. This means that at the unconscious level they are registering it, but because there is still conscious involvement, the conscious mind is not recognizing it. They may have a feeling that there something there, hints that something is taking place, but consciously it's difficult for them to register. You can tell if this is the case because you will see a strong positive state appear in your client even though they claim not to be able to see the symbol consciously. An easy way of getting around this is to simply ask them to close their eyes. Blocking out the visual sensory experience of the outside world allows them to get more into their internal experience. The act of closing your eyes induces a slightly altered state of consciousness because you are taking away a dominant sensory modality. When you're forced to switch modalities from visual to primarily auditory or kinesthetic, there is a moment of trance. This moment of trance is a doorway for the client to have a more unconscious experience. In most instances, when the client closes their eyes, the symbol will make itself apparent. Another alternative is to ask them to focus on how their body is feeling, and treat this as the new symbol.

You may also choose to frame the lack of symbol as being a symbol itself. The "nothing" the client is seeing may very well be the symbol they need at that time.

The other thing to look out for is a blending of the two symbols. If the previous two symbols have come together and blended in a way where each of the two previous symbols are still visible, the integration is more at the conscious level instead of an unconscious one. The client is consciously interpreting your suggestions and thinking that it means to combine the two earlier symbols. This is not as useful as creation of a new symbol by the unconscious; you are looking for the acknowledgment of the change to occur at the unconscious level. There may be some occasions where the blending of the two symbols will still work as a symbol for the reintegration, and you will know it when you see it because of the strong positive state it elicits. We are looking for the positive synesthesia between the symbol and the state, meaning the new symbol should lead the client into an even more positive state. Symbols are incredibly powerful in terms of human psychology and they have the ability to create and bring forth various states within us. Think about how you feel when you see a picture of a loved one, or an honored religious icon, or how it feels to see the logo of your favorite sports team; notice how your state changes. If a client gives you a blended symbol, if the emotional energy behind it matches that of the highest possible intention, then the symbol is useful.

Creating the Whole Person

Once both parts are integrated, the conflict has resolved and the unconscious mind has begun to generate new, resourceful ways of achieving its highest positive intention. Now it is time for the person to be reintegrated as a whole individual. This is the most powerful part of the reintegration process because it is a call to action for the client. The conflict has been symbolically, kinesthetically, and linguistically resolved and now it is time for the client to take responsibility for taking the change into the outside world, to take responsibility for the new state of their behaviors. To ritualize this transition, we have the client make themselves complete by integrating the new symbol into themselves, signifying the taking-on of the new state and behavior as a part of the client's normal everyday experience. This is also an incredibly powerful experience for the client as they fully take on the physiology of the new state.

This step is easy because your client will want to make the symbol a part of herself. That symbol is an anchor for the state, therefore the more the client has that symbol integrated into herself, the easier it is for her to access that state at any time. With the symbol in her hands, you can suggest the client both verbally and nonverbally bring that symbol into herself. Nonverbally you suggest this by gently touching the hands and suggesting through movement that they move toward the heart or chest. The client does not have to reintegrate this way, although it is a nice symbolic gesture that indicates she has taken the new state into her heart for her to carry everywhere. Some coaches like to suggest to the client directly that they take the symbol and move it into their heart. We prefer to be more ambiguous; perhaps the client needs that symbol somewhere else. For example, a client who had found the symbol of streams of light chose to move that light into his legs. Both of the client's hands, which had been in catalepsy, dropped straight down. For him, the purpose was action, and moving the energy into the legs meant that it was literally time to take action and move. Giving the client freedom to choose can be a valuable asset for them. The option is really yours as moving the symbol into the heart is also a very powerful and profound experience. Even when you are indirect with your communication, you will find that most clients will move it into their heart anyway.

As the hands are moving toward the heart, this is another opportunity for you to provide generative suggestions and linguistically suggest they take the symbol and make it a part of who they are from the inside out, a part of their whole being, a part of their everyday life. You can also continue to stack the nominalizations that the client had given previously and form suggestions for the complete integration of who they are as a person. Once you see the integration has taken place for the client, you can allow them to spend a moment enjoying the feeling of the new *them*. We like to suggest that only when they have the fullest sense of who they are now and all the possibilities available to them that they open their eyes and come all the way back to the here and now.

You can now future pace your client by having them imagine a time in the future when this new, fully integrated version of themselves will be useful. You can do this by applying the new resource, the new them, to the part of their life that was causing the conflict before. This is the beginning of the testing phase.

Testing

As the client orients into the world, this is a wonderful opportunity for you to reinforce the changes that have taken place. You can do this by first congratulating the client for having done such a good job with the process. When the client reorients, they're coming out of trance, and the first pieces of sensory information they take in will color the entire experience. Therefore it is important to greet them with a smile and make a positive comment.

Your role is to be completely congruent with the client's change. You have guided them through the process and you are certain that the change has taken place. It is your job to reinforce that certainty in your client. This does not mean you're trying to convince them that the change has happened — in fact, you want *them* to convince *you* of the change. But the certainty that you express as a coach is about maintaining space for the client.

Once they are reoriented, then you can begin testing. During this process you are still looking for their state, the emotional reaction. As you begin to ask the client about their feelings, continue to reaffirm unconsciously that change has happened, using nonverbal nods, smiles, and gestures. As the client thinks about the conflict, you are looking for a response at both conscious and unconscious levels. At the conscious, verbal level, you're listening for the client to have associated into the resource: "I feel confident!" or whatever the resource is. This means that they have decided to move in the direction of their goal in a toward-away problem. In a toward-toward conflict, we are listening for the ways in which the client has reached an emotional resolution with the situation and has found resources from both sides so that they can find new possibilities that do not negate either option. They will express this verbally and nonverbally. You're looking for the end state energy at this point. Are they still feeling conflicted, or are they accessing the feelings connected with the highest positive intention? Note that it is not necessary for them to have found a resolution to the conflict, although the integration of parts will make such a resolution inevitable eventually. Even if they decide to pursue one option and not the other, they can do so as a whole person, without internal conflict.

The best way to think of the testing phase is a cycle. You begin by gently asking the client to think about the context and how are they feeling. Once you have a positive reaction you can reinforce it by pushing a little bit harder. One way to do this is to ask them, "Are you sure that you've changed?" When they respond positively, you then ask, "How do you know?" The answer will be less in their verbal communication and more in the state that they convey; they will look totally congruent with their new way of being. Oftentimes as you cycle through this and really build their positive state, they may even become frustrated with you for not understanding how much they have already changed, and they may begin to "convince" you that this is a great place for them to be!

Coach: Welcome back. Great work! How do you feel?

Client: I feel good!

Coach: That's right. And when you think about discovering who you are, how does that feel?

Client: It's good.

Coach: And writing verses consulting . . .

Client: I can find out who I am while doing both. The consulting doesn't stop that.

Coach: It doesn't? Are you sure?

Client: Yes.

Coach: How do you know?

Client: Because I feel good!

Coach: Really?

Client: Yes! I feel great!

Coach: You do feel good! Is this a good place for you today?

Client: Yes, thank you.

To be truly masterful at the Visual Squash, you have to really practice discerning the client's unconscious communication. As an NLP practitioner and change worker, state elicitation is your most valuable resource. To be able to elicit the appropriate states from the client, and to be able to calibrate based on their unconscious communication, will set you light-years ahead of most coaches out there.

In the following chapters of this book we will cover alternative methods of using the Visual Squash, including a deep trance version, a conversational version, as well as the applications of the Visual Squash in business. Finally, we will cover how you can use it for yourself to create greater happiness and well being in your own life.

Receive your book bonus at www.visualsquashbookbonus.com

Chapter Eight: Deep Reintegration

In this chapter, we explore a version of the Visual Squash that is specifically designed to be used during overt deep-trance experiences.

The Visual Squash is a wonderful change-work pattern on its own, and it can also be used in conjunction with other NLP patterns, hypnotic interventions, or other coaching strategies. During a piece of change work, it may become apparent to the coach that a Visual Squash is the best technique to use. This may occur because of a conflict that the client presents, or because of a secondary gain issue that occurs within the parameters of the larger piece of change. When working with overt trance it is not always desirable to bring the client out of trance in order to do the Visual Squash, which will only lead them back into trance anyway. Because of the Visual Squash's covertly hypnotic nature, it is a powerful technique to use while the client is in trance, and can be done even when the client is experiencing the deepest levels of hypnosis.

When a client is in a deep trance it may be disruptive to the overall experience to have them open their eyes and engage in a more cognitive process such as the chunking up portion of the Squash. Also, why not take advantage of your client's incredibly resourceful trance state? Furthermore, an overt trance provides you with a number of resources that would have taken more work for you to elicit if the client were in a more uptime state.

There may also be times when it will be beneficial for the client to go into a formal trance before engaging in the Squash. If your background is in hypnosis as opposed to NLP, you may have a number of clients who expect overt trance. In fact, their expectation can be so strong that if they do not experience that overt trance, or if they are not consciously aware of the trance, the piece of change work you do with them will not be as effective.

Still another time when a more hypnotic Visual Squash would be preferable is when you're working with a deep trance subject. We will not go into detail here about deep trance subjects as it is beyond the scope of this work, but those of you seeing hypnosis clients will recognize this subject in that they have a very developed talent for going into and out of trance.

The transcript below is an example of how to use the Visual Squash when the client is in trance.

Coach: So, what would you like to work through?

Client: I would like to not drink as much.
Coach: Not drinking so much. OK. When was the last time you felt like you did drink too much?

Client: A week ago.

Coach: A week ago. And where are you?

Client: Um, I was over at a friend's house, and there was no purpose in the drinking.

Coach: All right. Do you want to stop drinking completely or are there times you would like to drink?

Client: I went out last night and just had soda water, so I know I can do it. It's a fact of going back home and being a part of my family system. They have bets on how to get so-and-so drunk, who's going to get drunk first.

Coach: OK, when you go home and you're a part of that family system, what is your ideal part of that system?

Client: Um, to go home, I don't mind having one or two,

but I don't want to sit down and have an all-day drinking event starting at 11 a.m.

Coach: And those times when there is a purpose to drinking, what are those?

Client: Celebrations. There are just too many of them, though. I have to pick and choose.

Coach: So how do you know which celebrations to honor with a drink and which ones not to?

Client: Hmm.

Coach: In the future, when you have made this change, which celebrations would you choose and which would you not?

Client: When we have a toast.

Coach: When you drank too much a week ago, what let you know you drank too much?

Client: I wasn't 100 percent. I woke up the next morning and wanted to do a whole lot of stuff, but it was hard.

Coach: OK. And once you've made this change, how will you be as a person?

Client: I'll be on my current track.

Coach: And what is that track?

Client: I'll continue working out, getting healthier, losing weight.

Coach: When you've lost the weight and are on the healthy track, who will you be as a person?

Client: Back to me.

Coach: And what is that feeling?

Client: It's great! There's a part of me that wants to this for myself. Then there is a part tied to my family. There is an obligation to be a part of their system

Coach: Can you be in the family and in the system and not drink?

Client: I can, but it will take a toll on me mentally. I have to prepare for any of their comments.

Coach: Does it have to take a toll on you mentally?

Client: Hmm. I guess it doesn't have to. That is what I don't want. I don't want it to take a toll. They'll make comments about me.

Coach: Are you prepared, then, that when you make this change, they are going to make comments? You get to be in a position where you take it on or you can leave it.

Client: I don't know yet.

Coach: That's right, you don't know yet. Are you willing to not know long enough to learn something new?

Client: Yes.

Coach: OK. So you have these parts, wanting to be a part of the family and wanting to do something for you. These desires on both sides are doing something for you. Even the behaviors we don't want are motivated by something good. Everything we do as people is motivated by some positive wish at some level. I think it is useful, then, to discover what that positive intention is so instead of you being pulled in two different directions, you can make the decision that is best for you having all of the information you need to make that decision. Does that sound good to you?

Client: Mmm-hmm.

Coach: Great. So if you could place your feet flat on the floor and your hands on your lap. That's it. And you've been in many trances before, have you not?

Client: Mmm-hmm.

Coach: I'd like for you to remember one of those times, recalling where you are and how it feels and where trance starts for you. Where does trance start for you

Client: My finger. [Finger twitches]

Coach: That's right, just pay attention to that finger. . . . And where does it go to next?

Client: My hand.

Coach: That's it. And what does that trance feel like? That's right. And that experience, that trance can begin to grow. There you go. [Client closes eyes.] And each breath you take can take you deeper inside. And the sounds around, noise from the outside can help you to focus deeply inside. The outside sounds reminding you that it's time to have an experience inside your unconscious taking you deeper now. Of course the sound of my voice will go with you on this journey because I know you are here to make a very important change. And in the past you had a behavior that you'd like to do less of and the wonderful thing to consider is that all you are is changing. Even at the cellular level you are changing. It happens so easily, old cells replaced by new healthy ones and you don't even have to think about it.

I know today you have your energy going in two different directions, one side of you wanting to be a part of the system and the other part of you wanting to make healthy changes, staying on the path. If you were to put that side of you wanting to stay on your current path on one hand, would it be your left hand or your right hand?

Client: My left hand.

Coach: Your left hand, making healthy decisions, being on your current path, doing something for you. So then this hand [gently touches the right hand] represents being a part of the system. And if you were to imagine something gently resting on this hand representing staying on the current path, what would it be?

Client: A flower.

Coach: That's right. And what represents being a part of the system, resting on this hand?

Client: A kitchen.

Coach: That's right, a kitchen. Earlier we spoke about both parts of you, the flower and the kitchen, each part of you having a positive intention, doing something for you. You may not know consciously just what that is yet. I'd like for your unconscious to begin going through all of the things each part is doing for you. So this hand here [touches left hand] can begin to rise only as quickly as your unconscious mind begins a search, inside, all of the wonderful things this part is doing for you. It can lift as it goes through all of the positive things this side wants for you. Now it may choose to let you know consciously or it could keep it secret. That's right . . . there you go . . . you're doing a great job . . . that's it.

Client: [Physiological shift as hand stops.]

Coach: That's right. . . . And this hand [right hand] can begin to lift as it finds that highest positive intention. While this hand [left hand] continues to hold on to that intention [indirect suggestion for continued catalepsy]. That's it . . . good . . . And your unconscious can choose to keep it secret from your conscious mind or it can let it know when it has discovered it. That's it . . . that's right.

Client: [Physiological shift and hand stops.]

Coach: Now I'd like for you to consider that each one of these sides has a certain skill, ability it can share with the other side. That's right. [Hands start to move together.] What skill does this side have that it can give to the other? [Touches the left hand.] That's right. [Unconscious nod.] And this side has a hidden ability it can give to the other side. That's right. [Unconscious nod.] And those hands can be in just the right position to share those skills . . . this side to this side. This side to this side. [Alternates between touching each hand.] And eventually when those hands touch, a new symbol will emerge signifying a new unified you. That's right . . . there you go. [Hands touch.] What is that? What do you see there?

Client: It's unity.

Coach: That's right, unity. So now you can make that a part of you. [Gently suggests hands moving toward her heart.] That's right. Unified being in the system while continuing on your path . . . having family and health . . . Now only when you're fully ready will your eyes open and you can return to the here and now feeling refreshed, relaxed, and fantastic!

Client: [Opens eyes.]

Coach: Great job! Let me ask you: when you think about the drinking, what happens?

Client: It's not there.

Coach: It's not there! And when you're home with the family on the holidays and they're drinking, what will you do? Something to consider: they are afraid. That's why they say things. They see you in control and they are not in control. They see you in control and it frightens them. They want to pull you down to them but you are much stronger.

Client: I can have a beer but I don't have to.

Coach: That's right, because you are in control and have that choice.
Client: [Strong positive state.]

The above example follows the standard format of the Visual Squash, however, there are some slight modifications. For the rest of this chapter we will be talking about some of the ways in which you can approach the Hypnotic Visual Squash in a way that maintains or develops a deep trance within your client while also eliciting the change they desire.

In this example we set out with the idea that this client would respond well with the mixing of both overt hypnosis and the Visual Squash. This is because we happen to know that she is a highly responsive hypnotic subject. She is also very associative, which means that she is able to step into states very easily. For this particular client, it does not require a lot of work on the coach's part to build up states. Therefore, most of this Visual Squash could be done content-free because we were sure that she was accessing the right states. She is also highly adept at catalepsy and hand levitation as a hypnotic phenomenon.

The first step of the hypnotic Visual Squash is found in the pre-frames that you set up with the client. Because clients tend to have an inhibition of speech during trance, it is very important that they are clear about, and accept, the frame that the unconscious mind only acts in ways that are for their benefit. Each part in a conflict wants something good. This is especially important when speaking about a toward-away problem. When a client consciously and unconsciously accepts these frames from the outset of the pattern, everything moves more smoothly. This is not to say that it is not important for the client to accept these frames before beginning a more uptime Squash; however, when doing the Visual Squash in trance, it is much easier when a client is clear on what to expect and the type of states that will be most useful in order for them to achieve a resolution of the conflict. We emphasize this because you should not have to bring the client out of trance in order to do the pattern. All change and all learning happen in a state of trance. To bring them out of that resourceful state could leave you at a disadvantage when it comes to doing the change work.

So during the pre-talk, and as you're discussing the context of the conflict, it's useful to layer up suggestions about each behavior being motivated by a strong positive intention. Just as when we presented some of the extremes of positive intentions behind behaviors, you too may find it helpful to illustrate this with your client using examples. If you separate the intention from the behavior it is easier to understand that the intention is good even though the behavior is problematic. As you're establishing these pre-frames for the Squash, look out for unconscious cues that the client has, or has not yet, accepted these frames (for example, nodding yes, shaking the head no, frowning, etc.). You may even want express your own curiosity about what the positive intention could be for the positive side. At this point you're not looking for the actual highest intention; you simply want to see that the client is thinking in the right direction. Something to keep in mind is that when you ask the client what they think, you are asking for conscious information. "Thinking," in the way the word is usually understood, is the realm of the conscious mind. This is not a bad thing, as you are just testing to see if they have the right idea, but it means that the highest intention will most likely not be presented at this point because the highest positive intention is within the realm of the unconscious. Remember, when you move to the conflicting part, finding the positive intention may take a bit more coaching on your end. The client may consciously have difficulty finding positive intentions. You can approach this the same way as you would when looking for the highest positive intention during an uptime Squash. Although you will most likely not reach the highest positive intention during the pre-talk and setup, you are formatting the mind to move in this direction. As we go along, having your client understand the process will be useful, especially if you are doing the work content-free.

In the following sections we present the moving parts of the deep trance reintegration. We assume that the appropriate pre-frames have been established. In terms of the actual induction, that's up to your discretion. You can either wait until the client exhibits a trance, as is the case when doing conversational hypnosis, or you can induce hypnosis using a classical induction, or in any way that you and the client are comfortable.

The Context

As you can see in the example above, no piece of change work is completely straightforward. Everything is a dance. When establishing the context in the example of the client with a conflict around drinking, some key statements stood out. The first is the idea of when it is appropriate to drink and when it is not. The client originally stated that it is appropriate to drink during celebrations. To the casual reader this may make sense — birthdays, holidays, or other important events. However, we have to be very careful with this because celebrations can happen at any time and any place. The client could celebrate the fact that it's a Saturday and use that as a justification for drinking. We have to be very clear in whether or not the celebration honors a person, an event, or if it honors the act of drinking. So it's very important to establish exactly how the client is going to know when it's OK to drink and when it's not.

The second thing that stands out is the idea of being part of a system. Initially it is not clear what she means by "being in the system." As we continue to explore this it becomes clear that, for her, the "system" represents being a part of the family dynamic. She does not want to lose her position in the family by making a change; however, she does not want her position in the family to be defined solely by drinking.

At first it appears that the purpose of the Visual Squash would be to integrate the part of her that wants to stop drinking with the part of her that wants to continue drinking. However, as we explore the issue further, it is clear that the actual parts that need to be integrated are the parts of her that would like to do something that is healthy and beneficial for her, and the part that wants to maintain her family relationships. What originally appeared to be a toward-away conflict is in reality a toward-toward conflict. This is very important to note because there is a secondary gain issue tied up in the problem. For this client, the gain is to continue drinking in order to maintain family relationships. That is a very strong gain from a less than desirable behavior. Approaching this from the point of view of a toward-toward conflict ensures a more congruent integration. While all problems have an element of secondary gain (otherwise we wouldn't be engaging in them), the question is: how strong of a secondary gain is it? Is the gain strong enough to maintain the problem regardless of the changes the client is seeking to make? In this case, the desire to maintain relationships in the family and to not have to deal with comments and teasing are very strong drives in maintaining the problem. Therefore this specific desire to still be part of the family system must be addressed.

Induction

Here we will talk a little bit about the specific induction we used in the example above. However, keep in mind that it's not really important what type of induction you use. You may find this type of induction useful for certain clients — or not. Our intention here is to simply shed light on the process of change that we used with this specific client.

The overt portion of the induction begins with establishing compliance through both an agreement set as well as requested behavior. We asked the client if she is willing to not know, whether she understands that every behavior has a positive intention, and if it sounded good to the client that both parts work together. The client agrees to the result of the Squash before we even begin the pattern. This establishes the client's compliance as well as indirectly placing the responsibility for the change on her. We then request that she put her hands on her lap and her feet on the floor. This request both puts her in a more stable and comfortable sitting position, and also is a continuation of the agreement set. Each request the client follows through on is the equivalent of her saying yes and each act of compliance is a small success. It also establishes physical compliance, which is useful since we will be using arm levitation.

The next question is in the form of a tag question: "You have been in trance before, have you not?" This both elicits another agreement and also implies that the client knows how to go into trance because she had that experience before.

We next invite the client to recall some time in the past when she went into trance. We want to revive that trance experience. The unconscious mind does not distinguish between what is strongly imagined and what is really occurring. Therefore, when someone remembers an experience, we can begin to build the state associated with that experience. In this example, we do this by first asking in the past tense and having her remember a time when she had that experience. We then shift the verbs from past tense to present tense, implying that it is occurring now. We also build the state by asking for specific details about where she is, when it is, and how the trance is starting.

Because this particular client is a skilled hypnotic subject, we know that it is only a matter of time before she begins demonstrating classic hypnotic phenomena. When we ask her where her trance starts, she indicates her finger, and as she does her right index finger begins to twitch. This is genuine unconscious movement. We know then that we have opened the door and it's only a matter of deepening the trance experience for the client.

The next part of the induction is *implication*. It is based on the idea that "where attention goes, energy flows." The more attention the client places on a particular experience or phenomenon, the more that experience tends to increase. Therefore we simply ask the client, "Where does that feeling move to next?" presupposing that it does, in fact, move. She states that it moves to her hand. From this point on we just build the experience by asking her what that trance feels like. This encourages the client to focus more deeply on her inner experience. It is not long after that when the client closes her eyes and drops completely into trance. As her eyes close, the physiological signs of trance deepen; her face softens, the shift in her breathing deepens, the ideomotor twitches in her finger continue, and she begins exhibiting REM activity (eye movements beneath her eyelids).

The next part of the induction is done with all our clients. There are going to be environmental sounds. We live and work in busy cities (New York and Philadelphia) where there is constant noise. Instead of having those sounds disturb the process, we use the "law of association" and tie the noise to a deepening of the trance experience. We use the client's breathing to do this as well. Everything that is in the client's experience can be utilized for intensifying trance and creating positive change. During the deepening process we also ensure that our voices follow the client to wherever she goes within the trance. This comes straight out of the work of Erickson, and the idea is that no matter where the client goes in her inner experience, we as coaches and guides will be with them. The sounds of our voices may change based on what's happening inside of them, but it will always be there.

Changing Loops

The induction is something that begins to transition the client from where they were to where they want to be. The first step of the induction is inducing actual trance; the next step is to imply change and to link change to trance in some way. It is not uncommon for clients to come to the session with the belief that change is not possible for them. This is because of how problems work: when a client has a problem, it exists because they have made it a static part of their experience. Often, they have turned the problem into a nominalization. Someone with anxiety, for example, will commonly say "I am anxious," as if "anxious" was their whole identity. Or they might say "I have anxiety," as if it were something tangible that they could possess — which, of course, it isn't. A key part of change is to take that nominalization and turn it into an action or process. Once the problem is put within the scope of an action or motion, the possibility of movement and change returns to it and it's no longer a static part of the person. When we do change work we take the nominalization the client presents, reintroduce it as action that has movement (i.e., a verb), and then finally turn it back into a static part of their experience, but this time in the past. They have frozen the problem in their present and future, and we unfreeze it, move it into the past, and refreeze it again. The client no longer "owns" anxiety; anxiety was a transient state, simply something they had experienced in the past.

Because your client may have spent a good portion of time nominalizing their problems, it can become difficult for them to believe that change can happen. If the client does not believe that they're capable of changing, then no matter what changes do take place, they might refuse to recognize them. This is why it is so very important to reintroduce to the client the idea that they can change. There are many different ways to do this. In this particular session, we chose hypnotic metaphor. Everything changes, our bodies change, the seasons change, tides change, and the phases of the moon change. If all of these things can change, so too can the client. The fact that they are changing at the cellular level all the time means that nothing can stay the same. This can be incredibly empowering for the client as they realize that the feelings are not permanent. Feelings only last a short period of time, 90 seconds, unless we are doing something inside of our minds to maintain them. When the client recognizes this, they will have more control over how they feel.

In the example above we introduced this idea through the use of metaphor and indirect suggestion, but you could choose to go a different route. Any way that you address the idea that "change is possible," and help the client to recognize change within her own experience, will work in this pattern. Your goal at this point in the process is simply to help the client recognize that they can control their feelings and resolve their conflicts in ways they have not considered yet. Even the word "yet" implies that a change is possible in the future.

The Visual Squash

Once the client is in trance and you have set the frames for change, it's time to assign the different parts to each hand. When asking clients in trance about the kinesthetic experiences, you'll often get an unconscious, nonverbal response well before a verbal one, or even in the place of a verbal response. This is an excellent time to use your calibration skills. When you ask the client which hand and they respond nonverbally using ideomotor signals (finger twitches, head movements, body shifts), the ideomotor movements may be very slight. It may only be in one finger and not the others. This movement may not even register to the client at a conscious level. In the example above, because we received both verbal and nonverbal responses, we continued to solicit the symbol; otherwise we would have first pointed out to the client that the conflicting part was on the other hand.

Eliciting the Symbol

This part of the process is identical to that of an uptime Visual Squash, with a few modifications. The first has to do with the physical nature of this pattern. In a normal Visual Squash, the symbol appears in the palm of the client's hand, but in this version it appeared on the back of her hand. To have a client sit with her palm up would make it more difficult to create arm levitation. It is much easier for the client to experience arm levitation when the hands are resting palms down, which is why the symbols was made to appear on the back of the hand. The same process is repeated with the conflicting part, in this case on the right hand.

The Dreaming Arm

The next step of this technique is based on Milton Erickson's "dreaming arm." The original version of this pattern involves the unconscious mind using arm levitation as an outward symbol of an inward search process. In this technique, the client is instructed to allow her hand to rise only at the same rate and speed that her unconscious goes through her memories, experiences, emotions, and dreams, finding all of the resources she needs to create change. The arm will begin to rise as the internal search happens. You may then suggest that eventually her hand will reach her face, and when it does she can have a dream. That dream can be a sign to her of the changes that have taken place. The dream communicates a new behavior, state, or understanding, or it may simply be a signal that her unconscious mind is involved in the process. After the dream has occurred, the hand begins its slow descent back to the client's lap. As the hand is going down, you can suggest that her unconscious mind can take all of those resources she has gathered and integrate them into herself so that in the future, she will have the state or behavior that she wants, when she needs it. As the hand goes down the coach may lead the client through a number of future paces in order to attach the resources to the times when they will be needed.

With this variation of the Visual Squash, we may use the foundational principles of the dreaming arm in conjunction with the Squash process. The client is instructed to allow the unconscious mind to carefully consider everything that particular part is doing for her. As that hand rises, it can continue going through all of those things until it reaches the highest possible intention, the strongest intention behind the behavior.

As a coach, it is your job to carefully calibrate the unconscious movements of the client's hand. You may notice that the hand will move up a few inches and then stop, pausing before continuing. It is almost as if the hand is actually stepping up through the different levels of intention. The clues showing that the client has found that positive intention are in her state change. Even if we do not know what that emotional change is, you will see it. Once you have calibrated that, you can confirm with the client that they have found the highest intention.

Now it's time to move on to the conflicting part, in this case, the right arm. The process is the same, although we are also calibrating for possible state changes in the wrong (negative) direction. If the state changes in a negative direction, then the client has either not accepted or simply not understood the pre-frames. You will need to go back a few steps. With the client in trance, her critical factor, the part of her that would normally interfere with finding positive intentions in the negative behavior, will be limited in its interaction. So it should be much easier to find positive intentions of the negative behavior in a deeper trance, although even in a deep trance there may be some residual conscious involvement.

The beauty behind this variation of the Squash is that we are leaving all of the responsibility in chunking up to the client's unconscious mind. This means two things. First, she will automatically find the congruent intentions for both sides. Second, the chance of chunking too far is diminished, because her unconscious mind will know when to stop. The client's conscious mind is not involved in the process, and the unconscious can sort for the intention far more quickly.

As the conflicting side is finding the positive intentions

and beginning the process of stepping up levels, you may notice something very interesting. When the conflicting arm has found the highest positive intention it tends to be physically at the same level as the resource arm, or close to it!

You may choose to have the client describe the positive intention — or you can instead choose to work "content-free." This means keeping it both out of your awareness as well as potentially outside the conscious awareness of the client. If it is outside of conscious awareness, the client's conscious mind cannot interfere with the process. This is where calibration skills are so important. If the client does not consciously know what the positive intentions are, she cannot explicitly tell you when she has reached it or if something is blocking her from discovering the intention. You must rely explicitly on the unconscious communication expressed through the arm levitation, and also gauge the client's state changes.

This experience is a powerful convincer for the client that she has an unconscious mind looking out for her, and that change can happen on its own. She gets to enjoy the change without interfering consciously, or knowing exactly how the change is happening. Think about it: how calming would it be to experience a change but not know how, only knowing that you have an unconscious mind that is always there looking out for you and capable of so many more things than you could imagine. This "not knowing" can be of tremendous therapeutic value.

How is it possible for a client to enact conscious control to create change on something they do not do consciously? The "not knowing" of how change happens is a wonderful metaphor for the new process: a resource trance as opposed to the problem trance. In the past the client would act out the unwanted state or behavior, but now they can enact the resolution and the new resourceful states and behaviors without having to consciously know how. This means they don't need to remember consciously when to do it — it simply happens when they need it to.

Hidden Abilities

Just as the highest positive intention may be kept out of conscious awareness, you can also keep each part's hidden abilities out of conscious awareness. Change happens at the unconscious level; the client's conscious mind simply catches up to the fact later. This is something you see time and again in change work.

Most of the time, you can clearly see unconscious processes happening. You suggest to the client that there are certain skills that each side has, and she will give you unconscious movements or signals that indicate not only that it is true but also that she has found them. Because you are doing this process primarily as a content-free piece of change work, the client will not be speaking about the skills that each side has to give to the other. Instead you will be looking for signals such as an unconscious nod, finger twitches and state changes shown in facial expression, skin color, and postural shifts. You are constantly calibrating the client's experience. The client that we have been using as an example in this chapter spoke about the skills that each side had as both of her hands began the journey of moving together. The unconscious mind is far more literal than the conscious mind, so you may see the hands begin to move together quickly when the process of gifting abilities starts.

As the hands move together, just as in the original Visual Squash, we encourage the client's unconscious mind to create a new symbol to represent her as a fully integrated person. When her hands touch she expresses an interesting symbol. Instead of something that would be visually related, such as the flower and the kitchen that she saw during the earlier part of the Visual Squash, this time her symbol is an idea: unity. We do not know what unity looks like to her, and she may not even know. She could see a picture or symbol representing unity, or experience unity in some other way. Whichever way she accesses the state is fine, and we know that the integration has been successful because it is embodied in her physiology.

Now it is time for the client to make unity an internal part of her experience. For this client, movement is unconscious and the integration happens very quickly. We suggest she opens her eyes only when she has a sense that that integration has completely and fully taken place at the unconscious level. This gives her unconscious mind the space and time it needs to complete the process. She can be assured consciously that, as her eyes open, the integration has taken place even before we do any testing of the new resource.

In the testing phase of the Visual Squash, we see a couple very interesting things happen. For this client, her goal was to cut down on her drinking, not to stop it. Her goal was to have a choice about when she did and did not drink and still maintain her family relationships. We first ask her about the drinking and she says it's not there. This indicates that the conflict is gone because the drinking is no longer at the forefront of her mind. Remember, this is about choice for her. This is typical in issues that are indicative of a Squash: the person is in a position of mutual exclusivity; they can only have one choice. The Squash is about creating ways to have the best of everything. And for this client, that is represented by getting the choice back in regard to her behavior.

The next step in the testing is to look at the family dynamic. We ask her what she will do when she's with family during the holidays, everyone's drinking, and maybe some comments are made. The client goes back inside to imagine the situation and apply her new resource. We took this opportunity to reinforce the work by giving her a different perspective, primarily what could be happening inside the minds of her family members who push her to drink. By giving this perspective we continue to build her resolve to have freedom of choice, as well as the confidence that she can do what is right for her. We set her above the family system in that she has an immense set of resources that they do not have. She becomes someone who is strong, independent, fearless, and who has the freedom to act and feel as she chooses. When she comes back out, after having done her own inner testing, she responds that she can have a drink or not have a drink. This is exactly the result she was hoping for, as opposed to feeling compelled to drink a large quantity to maintain her relationships and her position within the family system.

Notes

When doing a deep trance-style reintegration, at first it may go more slowly than an uptime Visual Squash. This is because, while in deep trance, it may take a bit longer for the arm levitation to happen and require more encouragement. If your client is particularly skilled at hypnosis and has many different trance experiences, it can go more quickly and sometimes even more quickly than uptime Squash. It really depends on the client.

Also, while a client is in trance there tends to be an inhibition of speech. This means that getting information about specific symbols or even asking them to chunk up out loud may prove challenging for them. There are two things you can do when this happens: suggest that the sound of their own voice will help them go deeper and they can speak with ease, and allow the client her own internal space to create the change. The latter is the example we used above.

Receive your book bonus at www.visualsquashbookbonus.com

Chapter Nine: The Content-Free Squash

In this next variation of the Visual Squash we build on the deep trance example, this time doing a content-free version. In the deep trance example, we had the context of the problem as well as the symbols. In the example below, we will not have any of those pieces until the end of the session. A content-free reintegration can be a very powerful tool, especially with a client who is reluctant to share details. There is an assumption that is made by many change workers that when a client comes in they will be willing to share everything with you, because they are there to change a situation. This is not always the case. A reluctance to share details may actually be the client demonstrating a piece of the problem to you. Even with your rapport-building skills, there are still some clients who want change, who are completely ready for that change, but who would like to do it within the privacy of their own minds! There is a difference between a client who comes in who is not ready for change and doesn't really want to give information and a client who is ready and actually on the edge of change but for whatever reason does not want to divulge too much. You will get a sense of both of these clients through experience. You will be able to tell through their state when they come in as well as their unconscious physiological communication.

There is something of a risk in doing a content-free Squash in that we do not have the context for the actual change, nor do we have any indicators of where the client is in the process intellectually. There is also the issue of ecology: as coach you will have the information based on their state, but the process of chunking up may not be completely clear to you. Therefore, just as in the previous example, we need to clearly communicate the idea of the highest positive intention with the client, and they need to be clear about what they can expect to experience.

This variation is a powerful tool, especially with someone

who is in touch with their own ability to shift states. The client in the previous example was able to move in and out of trance without a direct suggestions being made. In fact, for the change to have taken place at all he needed to go deeply into trance in order to access the resources, information, and the states required to resolve his conflict. Below you will find a transcript of the content-free Squash session; afterward, we explore the different nuances of this approach.

Coach: OK, so you have something you would like to work through.

Client: Yes.

Coach: Is it that one part of you would like to do one thing and another part of you would like to another thing, or is it that one part of you like to do one thing and another part of you would like to not do that?

Client: Part of me wants to be this way and then the other part just wants to be . . . One part of me wants to be helpful, another part of me wants to be angry.

Coach: OK. I'm going to pick up this hand here, and I'd like for you to go ahead and, in your mind, just assign to this hand one of those parts. You got it?

Client: Mmm-hmm.

Coach: Good. This hand over here can be the other part. And as you're considering both sides of the problem, imagine that on this hand there is a symbol, a representation, of just what that part is. Whatever comes to mind now, you can see it right here in your hand. That's it.

Client: Right.

Coach: In this hand is a representation of this part of you. There you go. Now, you know that each part of you wants something good for you even if you don't like the behavior.

Client: Yeah.

Coach: Just take a moment to be curious about what it is that side wants for you.

Client: Got it.

Coach: And you can also be curious about this side here. What does this intention have to do with this? There you go.

Client: Yes.

Coach: That's right. Now you can have an entire flood of skills and abilities moving through your mind from this part of you. All of the things that this part of you can do that this part over here really needs. That's right. And of course that means this side has some very important skills that this side over here needs. There you go. That's it. And each side, that's right, can give its skill, its ability to the other side. That's right, both sides working together. Already you have a sense of the changes taking place. One side giving skills to the other side. That other side helping the side to achieve that goal. Both sides wanting that positive outcome, those good feelings. And when these hands touch, you can come to a new understanding, and a new symbol can appear that represents the changes taking place at the deepest unconscious level. That sign, that symbol, that representation, is a new resource for you, something to carry with you to remind you of this at anytime you need it. That's right. That's it. And when you're ready, bring that symbol into you, making it part of who you are. That's it. And you can think about times in the future — maybe tomorrow, the next day, or next week — when the symbol, this feeling, can be so incredibly useful to you. There you go, that's it. You can think of another time, and a time after that, anytime after that.

And since you are in trance I would like to take a moment to remind you of just what an amazing hypnotic subject you are so that the next time you go into hypnosis you can go even deeper than this. You can be even more relaxed, even more comfortable. Because you're an amazing person, you really should have every opportunity to get the most out of every single hypnotic experience and have the opportunity to get the fullest out of every trance you have. That's it. So only as slowly as you're ready, your eyes can open and you can reorient to the here and now, as quickly as you would like to come out of trance.

Client: [Laughs.]

Coach: So, when you think about that problem, what happens now?

Client: It's good. I'm going to be more calm and patient. I'll be quick about it too. It's interesting because there was a pebble in this hand and a razor in the other, so I wanted to be sharp and quick. So I can be sharp and quick.

Coach: You have an incredible unconscious mind. You did a fantastic job.

Context

In this version of the reintegration pattern, we altered the ways we normally establish context for a problem. Because we are doing this completely content-free, the normal questions about when and where the last time this was experienced have been left out. Normally when we ask questions surrounding the context of a problem, specifically when and where the last time was that the client experienced the problem, we do so to understand the trigger for the negative state, and to help the client associate into that problem enough so that we can work.

Whenever we get the information surrounding a problem, we look for four specific things: the context, the trigger, the state, and the behavior. The context allows us to narrow down what in the client's experience is triggering the problem. All problems and solutions are found in anchors, and the trigger represents the environmental anchor for the unwanted state and, therefore, the behavior. The same applies for the client's resource state. During the change work process, we are using the old trigger as an anchor for the new positive state. When the context and trigger in the past would have set off a negative state and behavior, now they create a resourceful state and behavior. The heart of change work is in the "collapsing of anchors," resulting in attaching the resource state to the trigger.

Another reason for asking about the last time and place the client experienced the problem is to associate the client into the problem state. If the client is not associated into the problem it becomes exceedingly difficult to work with, and the change is more in the realm of the hypothetical. We might not have the fuel for the change to take place. To collapse the anchors, the problem anchor (i.e., the trigger) and the resource anchor need to be fired at the same time, so that when the client next encounters the trigger, the new state can replace the old. Please be aware that they only need to dip their toe into the problem — you do not want them to go too far into the negative feelings!

In this content-free version of the Visual Squash, the coach does not ask explicit questions about the context of the problem. Instead you are simply looking for state shifts in the client. We did this by suggesting to the client that they have a problem that they want to work through, and then we looked for a (negative) state shift. In this particular client we could see that he very quickly associated into that problem state.

If a client does not associate into the state easily you can still build it up by reminding them that there have been a number of times where they have had this problem . . . (and calibrating to their response) . . . that they can even remember the last time right now . . . (and calibrating to their response) . . . that they also know how it feels to be caught in that problem . . . (and calibrating to their response) . . . Use your language to help the client access that problem state. You can even tell the client you are going to ask a number of questions and they can answer in their mind without answering out loud. You would then go through the questions you normally ask to establish the context and wait for the state change.

As NLP practioners, we are not purists, we are pragmatists. Even doing a content-free Squash it can still be useful to get the parameters of the context, even if you don't have the specifics about the actual problem. This really depends on the client, how much information they are willing to volunteer, and how easily they access the state.

The Reintegration

This version of the pattern is very similar to the previous one so we will only mention here some of the important elements to consider. First is the importance of implication in this process. We do not have much specific verbal feedback from the client to work with, therefore we need to rely on state calibration to provide information about what is happening inside of them. Because of this, the coach's certainty becomes crucial. The client will have the symbol appear and they do understand the idea of highest positive intention. If they get lost somewhere in the process you will see it in their physiology. Confusion is a highly visible state in terms of BMIRs. Have confidence in your ability as a coach and your client's skill to make lasting positive change.

The second thing to note here is the variation in finding the positive intention for both sides. In this case we leave far fewer options for the client. We allow the client time to chunk up on the positive side until we see the state change to a strong positive. The client in the example above exhibited his states very clearly, so it was easy to tell when he reached a powerful positive intention. We also want to be sure that a congruent state is reached on the other, "negative" side, and cannot rely on verbal feedback. It is more challenging to coach the client to find that positive intention so we make it easy for them; in this version we ask him to consider what that highest positive intention on the resourceful side has to do with conflicting part. This question appears simple at first, but is actually deep and sophisticated in what it does for the content-free Squash: it presupposes that the positive intention is found somewhere on the more negative side, and it forces the client into a different type of search — they now need to go through their experiences to find all of the ways the conflicting side has been trying to meet that intention. This lessens the likelihood that the client falls into the trap of thinking that part is only doing negative things.

The rest of the Squash is straightforward; the one thing we did that was slightly different was future pacing in the pattern. As the integration occurred, we suggested that the client's unconscious mind begin applying this new resource to the future. We began with a small time frame, and then expanded it. This gives the unconscious mind opportunities to try on different ways of applying this new resource.

In the next chapter we will return to reintegration within a context, using a conversational pattern. The best part of this pattern is the client will not even be aware that a change is occurring at first. It will seem like a normal conversation, as if you are simply asking them some questions surrounding the conflict.

Chapter Ten: The Conversational Squash

This version of the Visual Squash is one of our favorites because it allows us to layer in Ericksonian (Milton model) language, conversational hypnosis skills, visual anchoring, as well as the coaching pattern. This version of reintegration is very useful when you're in a situation when eliciting catalepsy and doing a more downtime and trance-y Squash would not be appropriate. This version can be as conversational as you want it to be — it all depends on you and your client and your goals. This is a great pattern to use with friends and others who are not coming to see you for coaching. You can still be a powerful force for good and still use NLP patterns without it seeming like you're doing anything at all!

This pattern is also useful in the coaching settings when you have a client who is reluctant to experience anything that resembles formal trance, such as in business coaching. Of course, you can work around that by addressing the concerns, but you can also have patterns and skills available to you that work on a more covert level. The key to this variation is how conversational you can make it. This variation allows you to really explore your own creativity.

Coach: What do you want to work through?

Client: Food, I'd like to work on food.

Coach: OK, so talk to me about food.

Client: I'm really good with keeping the mindset of "food as fuel," but then I have my moments where it is, "Oh, my God

I've been so good, I need to devour everything."

Coach: When was the last time this happened?

Client: Wednesday.

Coach: Wednesday. Where are you?

Client: I was at a company event and they were passing around hors d'oeuvres, and food just kept on coming. They were small too, so it was like, "Oh, it's OK." I didn't think about it until I had an entire pile of the food in front of me. It is probably a lot more than I would normally eat.

Coach: So how is this a problem for you?

Client: Because I get up and do my workout, I barely eat anything all day. I mean, I eat small meals throughout the day, not how I eat when I want to devour things. Things are good, but then all of a sudden I'll want to snack. Then I'll get on the scale and see I haven't lost any weight.

Coach: That's how you have been. How do you want to be different?

Client: I want to see the numbers on the scale drop.

Coach: And what does it look like when the numbers on the scale drop?

Client: The numbers are going down, getting lower.

Coach: As those numbers are going down, lowering, how are you feeling?

Client: Like I have accomplished stuff.

Coach: Like you have accomplished stuff.

Client: Yes.

Coach: So when you feel that you have accomplished things, I'm curious, what does that do for you?

Client: It lets me know I'm on the right track and that I'm doing things for me.

Coach: And when you're on the right track and doing things for you, how are you feeling?

Client: Really good, really healthy, lighter.

Coach: And when you're good, healthy, lighter, who are you?

Client: I'm quicker and can do things for me.

Coach: That's right, you are quicker and can do things for you. How does that feel?

Client: It feels awesome.

Coach: That's right, it does feel awesome.

Client: Yeah.

Coach: What's it like when you have that awesome feeling?

Client: It's like being in the present moment, being in the now.

Coach: How awesome it is to be in the now!

Client: Yes it's like, *Namaste*. [Breathes deeply.]

Coach: So this other part of you that wants to snack when you've been good for a while, what is that doing for you?

Client: It's like little milestone rewards.

Coach: And when you have those little milestone rewards, how does it feel?

Client: It feels good, but it's weird. It's kind of in a negative direction. It's like, "Oh, I made it this far," as if I never believed I could so I'm giving myself a treat for just making it this far.

Coach: All right. So when you give yourself a treat for making it this far and it on some level feels good even when it has a negative side, what else is it doing for you?

Client: It's like I can start over. The next morning, the next day, it's a new day. Starts over.

Coach: I'm just thinking about those milestone markers as you celebrate accomplishments during your day — how do the treats fit in?

Client: They keep me going. I keep moving.

Coach: Keep you going and keep moving, what's that like?

Client: It's good because I'm moving away from old ways and moving forward to my goal.

Coach: Moving away from the old ways. And when you're moving away from how you used to be, what are you moving toward?

Client: Oh, I know what it is: "Yum." So when I get that food, it's that "yum" feeling.

Coach: You have that "yum" and are moving forward. How are you feeling?

Client: Good all over.

Coach: Ah.

Client: It's settling in.

Coach: Settling in. And what's that feeling even beyond that?

Client: It's like a vibration all over; it's like *Om*.

Coach: It's like *Om*. You can feel that *Om* all over, and is there anything after that?

Client: It's grounded.

Coach: That's right, it's grounded. And if you could go above that, what would that be?

Client: Oh! It's *Namaste*.

Coach: That's right. *Namaste*.

Client: It's about being in the now on this side too. I have no goals because I'm living in the now, and it's good.

Coach: It is about right now. So you have no goals, it's about the present moment, you experience *Namaste*. Isn't that interesting that you could have the same goal or non goal, the same intention for both sides?

Client: Yes.

Coach: That part of you that was doing the old behavior, I wonder what kind of skills it can give to the side working to achieve your goal.

Client: It keeps me grounded on a steady track.

Coach: Grounded and on a steady track. And that part of you moving toward your goal, what abilities does it have to offer that other part of you?

Client: I'll be going back home.

Coach: You'll be going back home. How wonderful.

Client: I have that *Om* and I'm going home.

Coach: So if you were to think about both parts of you at the same time . . . there you go . . . what comes to mind?

Client: [Laughs.]

Coach: That's right, what's that?

Client: Z*zz*. [Client makes a buzzing sound. Apparently for her the *Namaste* and *Om* sounds are the symbols representing each part, and the *zzz* is the sound representing the integration.]

109

Coach: It is that zzz. Is anything else coming to mind, or is it simply that zzz?

Client: It's the zzz.

Coach: Fantastic. So I'm wondering how you can take that zzz and make it totally a part of you and move it out into your future because that's an incredible resource you have.

Client: It is insane! [Client is laughing.] What just happened? I want to do it again! Let's!

Coach: OK, so think about your goal and the other part that was keeping you grounded at the same time.

Client: [Bursts of laughter.]

Coach: As you are feeling this, what's going happen the next time you're at the event and there are hors d'oeuvres?

Client: [Even greater laughter.]

Coach: There you go.

Client: It's like this zzz don't touch. [More laughter.] That is amazing!

Coach: Go ahead and think about those snacks and all of those milestones. What happens?

Client: Zzz . . . I can't touch [laughter], I go inside and say *Om*. It's like seeing an entire buffet of food with the red carpet and I'm running down the carpet and I'm only picking up the static.

Coach: And are you happy with that?

Client: Yes. I'm taking the zzz and the *Om* with me.

Coach: You did an absolutely awesome job.

The Meta Pattern

Before we jump into the mechanics of this variation of the Visual Squash, let's take a few moments to explore how change happens within the coaching relationship. Every single pattern in NLP — in fact, any successful pattern for change — follows the same basic structure. The structure leads to the collapsing of anchors before change happens, when the problem anchor is collapsed with the resource anchor. This is overtly witnessed when you do a standard NLP anchor collapse. However, it is also covertly present in every piece of change work. We cannot see change happen unless the resource is applied to the problem, and the client's neurology has the opportunity to apply that resource to the problem. Here we will briefly explore the structure of this process, which is known, in NLP, as the Meta Pattern.

The first step of the Meta Pattern is to associate into the problem state. You need the problem state to activate because you want to access the part of the client that has maintained the problem. To illustrate: when a client has a problem, certain neurons fire in their brain every time the client is introduced to the context and trigger of the problem. These neurons have been firing in the same exact pattern each time, almost like a closed loop. If you are going to change the way in which those neurons fire, you need to access them first. So we want the client to access the state as much as is appropriate. We do not need the client to dip into the state to such an extent that they are ready to abreact. Nor do we want them to exhibit the problem as fully as they experience it in the regular world. We only need them to access it enough to light up that neural pathway, and to recognize there has been a shift when the work is complete.

The next step of the Meta Pattern is to dissociate the client from that state. Now that we have that part of the neurology active at some level, the client does not need to be completely immersed in it. This is because it becomes very difficult to make a jump from the problem state straight into the resource state. It is easier when there is a break state in between to pull them out of that experience. The client is then in a better position to find the resources necessary to create the change. This dissociation can be done in any manner of ways. One traditional way is to do a classic pattern interrupt. This usually consists of asking the client a seemingly random question in a conversational way, such as "What are your plans for the evening?" Note that it should be a question that will not evoke a negative response, so don't ask about evening plans if they are working the night shift! This may also be done in a less conversational way by introducing a novel stimulus into the exchange such as a strange gesture or a loud sound. Gesturing and jokes, for example, are wonderful ways to break the state. Make the client laugh or smile, because not only does it break the state but it also puts them in touch with very powerful resource: laughter.

The third step of Meta Pattern is to associate into the resource. This means the client begins accessing the states that will be useful in overcoming the problem. For example, someone with stage fright may access a sense of confidence and relaxation during this stage. While in the first step we do not need the client to fully associate into problem state, in this third step when we do want the client to completely associate into the resource! The resource should be as big, bright, colorful, and powerful as you can make it!

The final step of the Meta Pattern is the collapse of the two anchors, applying the resource to the problem state. This is the point where we also get to test that the work has taken. This is the client's opportunity to test for themselves, and have a sense of achievement when they experience the resource state as opposed to the old problem state.

If we were to apply the Meta Pattern to the Visual Squash it would look as follows: the association into the problem is found at the level of belief in the conflict and the negative feelings that come from that. When a client comes in they have two mutually exclusive options, and the association into the problem is their belief that both options are mutually exclusive. This means they have to make a choice one way or the other, and there is going to be some sort of sacrifice relating to the option not chosen. This belief that the parts are mutually exclusive leads to the negative state; they feel bad because no matter what choice they make they will lose out on something. That negative state then leads to negative behavior, perhaps indecision or a lack of action. The client is caught between choices and cannot make a decision either way.

The break state or the dissociation part of this pattern is found in the assigning of the symbol for each part, as well as the experience of catalepsy. Both will be outside of the client's normal everyday experience; therefore both will draw the client's awareness from the problem state to this new phenomenon. This pulls them out of the problem state and "blanks the screen," so that they are in a much better position to make the move into the resource state. The placing of the symbols on the hands gives them the distance from the problem and allows them to work with it on a more metaphorical level.

Now is time to access the resource. The catalepsy itself tends to attract all of the client's conscious awareness and resources to that particular option, making it easy to find the highest positive intention. Once the states match on both sides (the positive intentions of each part are the same or at least aligned), the client has a powerful resource to go forward.

The final step of the reintegration, the collapsing of the anchors, occurs when the hands come together and the new symbol emerges. This collapses the spatial anchors that were set when each hand was assigned a part. This collapse also happens metaphorically. The two symbols come together and dissolve, giving rise to a new, more powerful resource. It is then time to make that resource a part of the client, pulling it into their heart and completing the reintegration. The result of this is a change in the belief; the parts are no longer viewed as mutually exclusive, but rather working toward a common intention. At the level of behavior, where the client was once hindered from taking action, he can now apply the resource state and the newly generated skills to the outside world.

We bring the Meta Pattern up at this juncture for two reasons. First, it is a useful way of conceptualizing NLP patterns. When you see all patterns within the context of the Meta Pattern, it is impossible to become lost in a piece of change work. This is important especially for those who are new to the world of change work. The second reason for mentioning it is that it is the cornerstone of the next step of the Conversational Squash. The Conversational Squash is based on the Coaching Pattern, which comes from John Overdurf, who also discovered the Meta Pattern in the form described above. When you understand the Meta Pattern, the Coaching Pattern becomes that much easier.

The Coaching Pattern

Just as an entire book could be written about the Meta Pattern, the same could be said about the Coaching Pattern. Here, though, we will keep the description short so you can gain a sense of what it is, the mechanics of it, and its application to this pattern.

The Coaching Pattern (as well as the Conversational Squash) relies on the use of conscious and unconscious communication. We communicate with the client's conscious mind through the use of language and with the unconscious communication at the level of gestures. We use gesturing in relationship to the client's timeline because that is where they spatially organize their past and future. .

The steps of the Coaching Pattern follow.

Step One: Establishing the Context

This is the standard opening in terms of change work. We ask the client what is it that they want to work through. Notice that we do not ask the client what they want to work *on* simply because that implies that they will not reach a solution. Working *on* something connotes a continuous process. We ask the client what is it that they would like to work *through*, which implies that they will reach a favorable solution.

We now associate the client a little more into the problem by getting the specific time and place. The client's initial response may be that this problem happens "all of the time" and "everywhere," but that is way too broad for us to tackle. We need a very specific time and place. When was the last time the client experienced this problem? Try and get this information as specifically as possible, down to the exact time, such as "Tuesday at 2 p.m. in the office." We then associate the client into the problem a little more by asking about what is happening. During this process there is a linguistic shift as we move from talking about the *last* time and place, in past tense, to speaking about the problem in present tense, as if it were happening now.

Finally, we want to chunk the client down to specific pieces of information. Primarily, we want to know the specific states, behaviors, and outcomes that are unfavorable for the client. An easy way to do this is to simply ask the client, "How is this a problem for you?" The answer that you are given will give you a great deal of insight into what it is they're doing inside of their own head in order to create this issue.

Step Two: Dissociating From the Problem

As the title suggests, at this point we want to break the client's state. We need to move them out of the problem mindset so that they can begin to access resources. We can do this very quickly by combining both verbal and nonverbal suggestions. Verbally we simply state to the client, "That's how you've been," while offering a nonverbal suggestion by moving our hand from the client's centerline to their left (the coach's right), usually low in their visual field. The movement is a type of "brushing away" of the problem. The implication here is that the problem is something that has happened in the past because, for a normally organized client, their past will be to their left or behind them and their future will be to their right or in front of them. You're both consciously and unconsciously moving that problem state from the present into the client's past. The client will consciously register this gesture as a part of the conversation. Unconsciously, however, they will understand the communication that the problem is in the past.

Step Three: Accessing the Resource

Accessing the resource happens in two parts, and, like the last step, it uses both conscious and unconscious communication. The first part of this process is to ask the client "How do you want to be different?" As we ask this question, we raise our left hand up to the top right corner of the client's visual field (the coach's left), palm toward the client. The unconscious mind for a normally organized person accesses creative images by looking up and to the right. We are inviting them to make a picture of their ideal outcome. When we move our hand to visual-create, most clients will track the movement with their eyes; this makes it easier for them to create that picture. We can then ask them specifically what it is they see or simply wait for the response of how it is they want to be different.

The client will give a description of the state, perhaps, "I want to feel confident!" (if confidence is their desired state). As they do that, we move our left hand down and toward their heart (obviously without touching them or invading their personal space), as if we are gently pushing that outcome inside of them. As this happens we ask them what is it like when they are feeling their desired state — "What is it like when you feel confident?" This continues the process of building the resource state. The client will then continue to give you a more detailed description of the particular state or resource that they would like to have.

Step Four: The Collapse

The final step of the Coaching Pattern is the collapse of the resource state with the old problem anchor. After we have built up the resource state, the client is ready to apply it. The unconscious communication during this phase is very similar to the last: we reaffirm the client is experiencing the state inside of them by gently gesturing. Once again, the client will consciously recognize this as you simply using your hands as you have this conversation when in fact you are guiding your client to apply the resource. An easy way of doing this is by saying to the client, "And as you are feeling confident, think about that old problem [gesturing down and to their left, where we left the problem] and notice how it is different." Because problems cannot stay the same once new information enters the unconscious, it will have changed. There may be a slight change or, in some cases, the problem may be blown out then and there.

The Coaching Pattern is a very direct and explicit example of the Meta Pattern in action. We have explored it here because the Coaching Pattern is the foundation of the Conversational Squash. You will notice a slight variation in some of the steps; however, the general maneuvers and the unconscious suggestions used within the Coaching Pattern are essential elements of a conversational reintegration. Because the conversational reintegration is just that — conversational — we need to use naturally occurring gestures and language to elicit the states and create the collapse. In this version of the pattern we will not be using catalepsy, nor will we be asking the client explicitly for the symbols. In terms of the symbols, we will create them unconsciously for the client. As we go on, we invite you to keep the Coaching and Meta Patterns in mind as useful ways to understand the Conversational Visual Squash.

The Conversational Squash

All four steps of the Coaching Pattern are embedded within the Conversational Squash and are important techniques in establishing the different aspects of the Squash. We begin this process by getting the context of the problem; specifically the last time the client experienced their issue. When we ask the client when and where, most will access visual recall (looking up and to their left, for a normally organized person). The image they pull up becomes the symbol for the problem state. Unlike in the normal Squash, where we begin with the positive state, in this version we start with a negative state, the conflicting part because this is exactly what the client presents us with. If we want to maintain a conversational flow, to ask the client to find a representation for it may seem a bit strange and out of context. So the memory itself of the last time and place that they experienced the conflicting part becomes the symbol for that side.

We now break the state in the same way we do in the Coaching Pattern, by moving the problem, the memory, into the client's past while affirming that that is how they were. This is a nice conversational way of assigning that part of the conflict to the left side of the client. Although we will not be utilizing catalepsy of the hands, we will be using spatial anchors: the problem is moved to the client's left side, your right side if you are facing them, and the resource appears on their right (your left).

Accessing the resource state is not to be confused with the highest positive intention. By *resource state* we simply mean the more desired of the two outcomes. Just as in the Coaching Pattern, once again we do this conversationally by directing the client's gaze into visual-create by asking how they want to be different. They will make a visual representation of the desired outcome. In the example earlier, this was the image of the scale with its numbers going down.

You are now in a good position to begin chunking up. You have the conflicting symbol on the client's left and the resource symbol on the client's right. They probably are not even consciously aware that you have separated the sides of the conflict for them. To chunk up, begin with the positive part. We already have the client in the resource, so instead of jumping back to the conflicting part, it is more natural to stay on topic.

The chunking up process is similar to the chunking process in any of the other Squashes. The only thing to keep in mind is that because this is a conversational pattern, you want to vary the ways in which you ask questions. This is where your artistry as a conversationalist comes into play. You can keep chunking up by asking varied questions about each level of the chunk.

> I wonder what is that doing for you?
> What do you have when you have that?
> How is that helping you to be the person you want to be?

And so on. Eventually you will see the state shift and know that you have reached a high enough chunk. The same holds true for the conflicting side. Think of this portion of the reintegration as a type of brainstorming: what can the person get out of both of these parts of themselves? You can ask: "I wonder what that is doing for you? It must be doing *something*." Explain to your client that they are intelligent and resourceful and you know that there's something in both those parts that contains skills and abilities.

What would happen if the client were to think about the two symbols at the same time? That is, they think about the memory of the last time the conflict took place, but also how they want to be different. In the above example it was the memory of the party as well as the image of the scale. Your job is to pull both images in front of them. So with your right hand moving the symbol from their past and with your left hand moving the symbol from their visual-create space, they both appear in the space directly in front of them. This is the collapse and there will be a neurological response, a dissonance, as they attempt to maintain both pictures, the old state and the new positive intention, at once. During this collapse the deck is stacked in your favor. Not only do you have the resource state and the positive image, but you also have that intention that applies on both sides. This is why in the example above the client expressed a visceral response. It was a feeling that she could not put into words. Afterward, each time she thought about those pictures or the behaviors, she had the same positive reaction. The collapse was complete.

Now that the reintegration has taken place you can test for results. Ask the client to imagine a time in the future when they may experience a conflict and notice what happens. Through this testing process you also reinforce that new state. With the client above, the more we tested it, the stronger the response became. Think of it as conditioning the new response.

You can make this version of the reintegration as covert or

overt as you like. In the following chapters we will examine the ways in which you can use the Visual Squash in other contexts.

Receive your book bonus at www.visualsquashbookbonus.com

Chapter Eleven: The NLP Negotiation Pattern

The principles of the Classic Visual Squash pattern essentially involve the negotiation between two parts of the client's mind. Each part is asked to specify its positive intention, what it values, its goal or highest intention. Once each part has specified its highest intention, then the hypnotist or coach seeks some form of overlap, some common positive intention, shared by both parts. Once the highest positive intention is identified it can be used to drive new behaviors in each part. The parts then become allies in dealing with the decision at hand.

Therefore, the Visual Squash is a value negotiation between the two parts. Each part specifies what it values most, what it really wants from the negotiation, so the common ground can be found. It is not surprising that the principles of Visual Squash can be used to create a framework for conducting negotiations between two parties, simply by treating each of the parties as part of a larger system. We describe how the principles of the Visual Squash can be used in negotiations in this chapter.

Why Negotiate?

We negotiate with another party in order to get something they have that we want in exchange for something we have that we are prepared to give up. This is a question of value. In order to have a successful negotiation I must value what they have more than I value what I have, and they must value what I have more than they value what they have. If this is not the case, then no successful win-win negotiation is possible. I am better off because I get something of more value to me than I give up. They are better off because they get something of more value to them than they give up.

Another way of thinking about a negotiation is that both parties put all their resources (or at least all the resources involved in the negotiation) into the center of the table and divide them between the two parties. I will be putting resources into the center of the table, and while they have limited value to me, they potentially are of greater value to the other party. The other party will be putting resources onto the table, and they have limited value for them and potentially greater value for me. By dividing these resources between the two of us, we are each able to walk away from the table richer than we came, a sort of alchemy where my lead is turned into their gold, and vice versa.

Unfortunately, some people treat a negotiation not as a search for values, but rather as a confrontation or competition. If I win the negotiation, the other party loses. If they win, then I lose. The win-win nature of a negotiation can be lost in the shuffle. In this case, the negotiating points become pawns on a competitive chessboard; as a player in the negotiation, I come to value each and every pawn and will give it up only at great cost to my opponent. This will be my position even if the pawn has little or no value to me. Using this competition metaphor for thinking about a negotiation, I focus on the pawns and pieces I have to negotiate with, rather than the value I am seeking. This approach may not only damage my opponent, it may also hurt me, because I may insist on keeping hold of something of no value to me because it has great value to my opponent.

What Is a Win-Win Negotiation?

A win-win negotiation is very different from a negotiation in the form of a competition.

In a win-win negotiation each party actively seeks to bring as much value as they possibly can to the other party. They seek to find resources that they have, that bring limited value to themselves but greater value to the other party. Once they find such resources, they happily give them up to the other party knowing that they are also seeking to bring value to them in return. In contrast to a competition negotiation, in a win-win negotiation each party is working on behalf of the other party, secure in the knowledge that the same thing is happening on the other side. Both parties are seeking to maximize value.

Imagine that you receive a cold call from an Internet marketer. This gentleman spends his time on the call talking about two subjects: the deficiencies of his competition, and how much he wants you to sign up with him as a client. Never once during the conversation does he ask you about your needs or about how you define value for your business, or how he could help you to find that value. Needless to say, you probably would not be attracted by the services he describes.

A win-win negotiation can have several important advantages over a competition negotiation. In a competition negotiation I'm seeking to maximize my own value at the cost of minimizing the value I bring to my opponent. I have two aims: to maximize my own value, and to minimize his. He has two aims: to maximize his value, while minimizing mine. Because our energies go into minimizing the total value, the total value is going to be less than it otherwise could be. In contrast, in a win-win negotiation, both parties seek only the maximization of value. Therefore, in a win-win negotiation, it is likely that the total value of our "pie" will be greater than in the competition negotiation.

In the competition negotiation it is likely that my opponent will view me as his opponent. There could be feelings of ill will on each side. This can lead to buyer's remorse. In contrast, during a win-win negotiation, my partner will have the feeling I'm working actively on his behalf. It is much less likely there will be animosity or buyer's regret. Therefore, in a win-win negotiation, repeat business for both sides is likely. The best salesmen are not the ones who drive the hardest bargains, but rather the ones who develop high value continuing relationships with their clients and customers.

Clearly, a win-win negotiation can only take place in the context of trust and respect between the parties. In the absence of trust and respect, I seek to win by making my opponent lose and vice versa, and we fall back into a competition negotiation.

Applying the Principles of the Visual Squash to Negotiations

When you are involved in a negotiation, either as a neutral arbitrator or as an interested party, you can use the principles of the Visual Squash in order to reach a win-win solution that benefits everyone involved.

The first step in the Visual Squash is of course to identify the two parts, which are seemingly in competition, and to build initial rapport between them. To build it, reframe the negotiation in a way that the needs of both parties can be satisfied. The concept of fairness implies a win-win outcome for both parties.

The second step is to define the initial requests of each party — what they say they want. In this case, we know who the parties are, so our first step is to simply ask them what they are looking for in the negotiation. The answer may be general or specific. In either case, the client will say things like:

"Value for money" or perhaps "I'm not prepared to pay more than $100."

"Good quality" or perhaps "Two references and a bank guarantee."

"I need it done soon" or perhaps "Phase 1 must be completed by the end of the month, and the entire project completed by the end of February."

The next step is to discover the underlying values upon which the demands of each party are based. Whether they say "Value for money" or "I'm not prepared to pay more than $100," we do not know what the motivation is. For example, what do they mean by "value for money"? Is this based upon the price of the product compared to competing products? Or is this based upon the quality of the product? And if so, how is the monetary value of a superior product compared to the monetary value of an inferior product? And what are the qualities of the product that would make it superior or inferior? Why are they not prepared to pay more than $100? Do they have a budgetary constraint? Or have they seen another product that matches their needs and sells for $100? If so, is that product or at least equal in quality to the one they are negotiating for? Until we gain a greater understanding of the values that underlie the demands, we do not know how to maximize the total value to both parties.

Let's consider an example relevant to you as a coach. You provide solutions to your clients' real-world problems. What you give up is time. In order to bring value to your clients, the value you place on your time has to be less than the value of the solution that you bring to them. As long as the monetary value of your time is less than the value to your client of the solution you provide, then a win-win negotiation is possible. If a client approaches the negotiation as a competition, then rather than focusing on the amount of value that your solution brings to them, they will focus instead on the amount of time you spend to provide the solution, and the cost of this time, and therefore of the solution, to them. If you're able to provide a solution quickly, then from their perspective within this competitive frame, you should not charge very much because you haven't had to give up time. It is like the story of the engineer who was brought in to fix the very expensive machine. He turns the machine on, listens to the groaning noise it is making, then taps it with a hammer on a certain point and fixes it. He hands a bill for $10,000 to the owner of the machine. The owner of the machine of course requests an itemized statement and the engineer resubmits his bill as follows: "Tapping on the machine — $10. Knowing where to tap — $9,990. Total — $10,000."

Having discovered the actual underlying values that each party has in the negotiation, we can seek to maximize the total value of the negotiation, and by doing so maximize the value for each party. Keep in mind the criteria or aspects of the negotiation that are most critical to each party, and which are of only limited value. For example, in the consulting world, clients authorize payments under their budgets. They might see the value of a coach's services, but if they had already spent their budget for the year, they might not be able to pay. But perhaps the coach could wait for payment until the following year, when the client has a new budget and could afford the work. The critical concern of the client is not the amount of the fee, but when the fee was payable. By offering to wait for payments until the following year, the coach could increase value to them by allowing them to use the following year's budget, at minimum inconvenience to herself. In this way, value is maximized for both parties.

In practice, this means that you can be happy to offer something that is of small value to you, and great value to your negotiating partner. It increases the level of rapport within the negotiation, and in exchange for your concession, you can expect your negotiating partner to work on your behalf by offering something important to you. Link this to your concession by saying something like, "I know how important it is for you to have x, so I think I can see way to get that for you . . . and I would be very happy to have y, would that be possible?" By the time the more difficult pieces of the negotiation are reached — the things that are important to both sides — a great deal of trust and rapport has been built and both sides are deeply invested in the process.

Once the terms of the negotiation have been agreed upon, it is good practice to give the other party something extra, something additional, as a symbol of this win-win attitude. This will ensure that they leave the negotiation feeling good about the process and about you. This is a great way to build repeat business.

Choosing Between Exclusive Options

In coaching, the Visual Squash is often used to deal with the type of problem called Exclusive Or's. Exclusive Or's are alternatives where we can either have alternative A, or alternative B, but we can't have both at the same time. The alternatives are said to be exclusive because having one excludes the possibility of having the other. For example, a client may wish to stay in their current job, and on the other hand they may wish to pursue a new career. These two alternatives are mutually exclusive. The client becomes torn, unable to leave yet unhappy about staying.

The Visual Squash works by chunking up from a behavior to a value. Alternative A provides value A, and alternative B provides value B. For example, pursuing your dream job might give you career satisfaction, but staying in your current job may give you security. Certainly if you pursue your dream job you lose the security of your current job, but you do not necessarily lose all job security. And if you stay with your current job then you do not necessarily lose the possibility of job satisfaction as long you are prepared to negotiate changes with your employer. Space has been created within the seemingly exclusive possibilities: you can find a way to be secure pursuing your dream, or find a way to pursue job satisfaction within your current career, or pursue a third role that provides both security and job satisfaction.

Thus the Visual Squash can also be used in a business

context to choose between seemingly exclusive alternatives.

How We Make Decisions

We make a decision to take a certain action because it gives us something we want. However, we often misunderstand what it is that we actually want. For example, someone may spend their life working extremely hard in order to make money, and therefore assume that what they want is money. In fact, money is simply a means to an end. What money does for us depends upon the individual; for some people, money represents security, for other people it represents achievement, for others it represents freedom. Each person seeks a different value (security, achievement, or freedom) through the medium of earning money.

Very often we fail to consider what our true needs and values are. Instead we consciously focus on something that we unconsciously hope will bring us those values. The Visual Squash allows those true unconscious values to be brought to the surface and begin to act as the explicit drivers of behaviors and choices.

Exclusive Alternatives

Our inability to recognize our own true values can lead us to unnecessary difficulties in the case of exclusive alternatives. For example, if a business owner lets go of some of his sales staff and at the same time asks the remaining sales staff to make the same number of sales calls as before, he will then wonder why he later loses his best salespeople to burnout, and why the remaining sales staff became disheartened and sales go down.

By focusing on two different behaviors that are mutually exclusive, you can put yourself into an inescapable bind. Instead, if you focus on the value that each behavior provides, you'll find a more balanced solution. In the above example, suppose instead of letting his sales staff go, the business owner focuses on the reason he wants to let them go ("What does this do for me?"). Once he knows what value is truly being satisfied, he may build to find a solution that gets him everything he wants without the adverse side effects.

Seeking the Positive Intention

In order to find the true values that drive our decisions, we need to ask ourselves "What does that do for me? Why do I want that?" Once we have found the real answers to these questions then we are no longer left with one alternative and one alternative only. There are many ways to achieve our true goals and reach our true values.

We need to ask these questions on a repeated basis. For example, if a client decides they would leave like to leave their current job, they may explore the following reasons for this decision:

Coach: Why would you like to leave your current job? What does that do for you?

Client: By leaving my current job, I would have time to pursue my writing.

Coach: And when you have time to pursue your writing, what does that do for you?

Client: When I pursue my writing, I may complete and publish my book.

Coach: And when you have completed and published your book, what does that do for you?

Client: When I have completed and published my book, I will have the recognition I deserve as an author.

Coach: And when you have the recognition you deserve as an author, what does that do for you?

Client: When I have the recognition I deserve as an author, I will be happy.

So in this case the positive intention is to gain happiness. Rather than worrying about whether or not to leave their job, your client can instead focus on pursuing happiness in all its forms!

When we have found the true values that drive our

decisions, then the problem of Exclusive Or's may disappear.

Applying the Visual Squash to Logical Decision-Making

When you reach a point in your professional life where you have to make a decision and the results of that decision appeared to be a lose-lose outcome ("damned if I do and damned if I don't"), then it may be time to use the principles of the Visual Squash.

Look the two alternatives you are considering: You can have alternative A or alternative B, but not both. Select the alternative that appears to be more positive. By *positive* we mean the one that appears to satisfy your higher needs, your yearning for freedom or adventure. Which one are you most attracted to?

Once you discover the one that is the more positive, let's say it's alternative A, begin to seek the positive intention of A: what does it do for you? When you've answered this question, ask yourself "And what does that do for me? What do I have if I have that?" Continue asking these questions until you have fully explored the benefits of alternative A and the values that underlie that alternative. You will know the process is complete when you cannot find a higher benefit, or a higher value, then the one you have identified. When you can find a higher value but it seems distant and theoretical and does not attract you, there is no emotional attraction to that value.

Repeat the process with alternative B.

You may find that you get a high value that is shared by both alternatives A and B. This will be the highest shared value of the two alternatives. You may find you do not find a value that is shared between alternatives A and B. If the highest value of alternative A is value A, and the highest value of alternative B is value B, ask yourself "What would I have to have in my life that, if I had it, I would automatically have value A and value B?" In this case, this will be the highest shared value of the two alternates.

Once you have the highest shared value of the two alternatives, ask yourself what you can do, what options you have, that will lead you to having this highest shared value. Once you've found this option, you will know what is right because you will have the feeling from both parts of you that this is the shared value.

128

Now begin to ask yourself how the values of alternative A can inform, help, and assist the values of alternative B, and vice versa. This will continue to build a sense of rapport between the two alternatives. The two alternatives will become mutually supportive rather than mutually exclusive.

Receive your book bonus at www.visualsquashbookbonus.com

Chapter Twelve: Self-Reintegration

As coaches we can forget that the same techniques that we use to help others can create lasting happiness in our own lives. In this final chapter, we're going to build on the ideas presented in the rest of the book by exploring two different ways in which you can use the Visual Squash for yourself. The first way is a cognitive approach. In this version you'll be actively searching through your experiences to access the proper states, which will trigger the reintegration. The second version is a more hypnotic technique in which you will rely on your unconscious mind to create the changes. For those not familiar with self-hypnosis, we provide a short technique that you can use to access trance.

Cognitive Reintegration: Assigning the Parts

Being that it is you who has a problem to solve, setting the context can be explicit. You are the one experiencing the conflict, so you know when and where it happens. You can simply think about the conflict in that specific context and have an awareness of how your state changes in response.

Assigning the parts becomes interesting because any issue can be toward-toward or toward-away depending on how it's framed. When working with clients, we tend to use whichever way they frame the conflict. When working with yourself, you will have a sense as to which form of the conflict is more understandable. Are you attracted to both options, or attracted to and repulsed from one outcome at the same time?

You may want to assign the parts to sides, or to hands,

although in this version of the reintegration, catalepsy is not necessarily needed and we will not be relying on it. Of course, if you are in a very deep trance, feel free to ask your unconscious to perform a full-on content-free reintegration for yourself! We discuss ways of doing this in the hypnotic section below.

In any case, because we are working more at the cognitive level, you can work with one part at a time; there is no need to assign hands or even symbols. In the case of the self-reintegration, the symbols you will use are simply the ways in which you think about those parts. You may find that one part triggers a memory and another part triggers a daydream. However you represent those two parts within your internal experience is perfectly fine and valid.

As previously mentioned, one way of conceptualizing the reintegration is that it is a negotiation. Both parts of you want what is in your best interest. As you go through this cognitive process, keep in mind that you are overseeing a negotiation within yourself where it is in your best interest to have a win-win outcome. This means that no matter which direction you go in with respect to the conflict, you know that you have resources and skills available to realize a positive outcome.

Chunking Up

As you begin chunking up, just as when you are working with a client, you are sorting for the best possible state. When you take the time to focus on your own experience, you will be aware of when your state has shifted. This requires paying attention to how you feel as the process unfolds.

Similar to when you are working with a client, we recommend beginning with the more positive part because it is easier. As you start chunking up, have a feeling of curiosity as to what the part is doing for you. You are an amazing person and the fact that you have these two parts shows your mind's resourcefulness. Having these parts allows you to see both sides of the issue, so why not be curious about just what motivates those parts? Because this is more cognitive, you will find a number of ideas and nominalizations coming to mind. Do not become attached to any one of these, but simply allow the process to continue and keep being curious. You will find at first that some of the nominalizations do not carry a strong emotional charge. These will be more like ideas, thoughts that never crossed your mind until now, as you consider the particular part. The higher you chunk, the stronger the emotional charge will become. You will know that you've reached a high enough chunk when you've noticed a distinct state shift. You may even have a part of you say, "Yes, this is it!" If you notice the emotional charge reducing, then you may have chunked up too far, into abstraction. Take it back a couple of steps and notices what happens.

If you are more oriented toward a "thinking" experience, engaging in self-talk, then you can simply ask yourself "What is the intention behind this?" Begin to chunk up in the same way in which you would chunk up with a client, by asking yourself questions and waiting for the state change to occur. If you are more visually oriented, then it may not be words that are the best medium. Instead, you may find yourself going through a series of internal images until an image elicits a strong enough state change that you know this is it.

If you are someone who has a much stronger kinesthetic bias, the chunking process will be slightly different. While self-talk and visually oriented people are using nominalizations or imagery to cause a synesthesia for the state, you can sort directly for the state. You'll know you've reached the highest positive intention when the state is at its strongest, when it peaks. That state then becomes the driving force behind the entirety of the reintegration.

Finding Hidden Abilities

This part is also quite straightforward. You're using the same strategy as you would with the client. You can be fascinated by the fact that each part of you has certain invaluable abilities. You may even find yourself, as you think about each part, daydreaming about times and places where the skills of that part will be useful. As a coach you are in a unique position because you have already fully accepted the pre-frames of this pattern. That means the chunking process, and the searching for hidden abilities, will be easy and more straightforward!

Reintegration

This part requires active involvement of your unconscious mind, so you will be using your imagination. Have the positive side pick one of the skills and move it to the conflicting part. As you think about the conflicting part, imagine how that expresses itself differently now that it has this ability. Next, choose one of the abilities from the conflicting part and apply it to the positive side. You can imagine what it will be like when this positive side has the same skill that the conflicting side possesses. You can go through this process for as many abilities and skills as you have for each part. For the reintegration, we are weaving these skills together. You are taking a positive part and internalizing it on the conflicting side, and then taking the skillfulness of the conflicting side and internalizing it for the positive part. You go back and forth until you have explored all of the skills for both sides.

The final step of the reintegration is generating new ways in which you can meet the highest positive intention. Remember, the problem does not come from the fact that you have conflicting parts. The problem arises when there is a belief that both of those parts are mutually exclusive. The negotiation that happens between parts is to establish that they are not exclusive. Not only that, but there are countless other ways that you (and the parts) can achieve your goal without losing important aspects of either part. So now that you have the highest positive intention and a variety of skill sets, you can be curious about just how you can reach the positive intention in different ways.

This portion of the reintegration requires you to use your imagination again. Your unconscious mind knows what direction to take you because it knows the end state energy that arises from the highest positive intention. Your job is to create a plan — to strategize new ways in which you can attain that feeling. These new ways may include elements of each part or you may find that you're generating completely new ways of doing this.

For example, suppose you have a conflict where part of you wants to leave the job and the other part of you wants to stay. The highest positive intention in this example is happiness. You may begin to generate a plan to increase happiness while staying at the current job, perhaps by spending more free time pursuing your interests. On the other hand you could increase happiness by changing jobs into one that is more rewarding, stable, or in alignment with your values. A third option could be to recognize that happiness is an internal state and thus reliant on you and not external circumstances. Of course there are many other ideas and thoughts that could be generated; this is simply to illustrate some of the possibilities of including the parts or moving beyond them.

This version of the Squash is highly cognitive but you are using some unconscious processes, including your imagination, though for the most part this is kept at a conscious level. If you come from a hypnosis background, you may have more of a bias toward the unconscious; however, with NLP, change can happen through a cognitive approach as well as through the door of the unconscious. No matter what, for change to take place, both the conscious and unconscious have to be involved. Whichever way is more comfortable for you will give you the better results.

In this next part we will look at a more unconscious version of the Squash, which you can use coupled with self-hypnosis.

Hypnotic Reintegration

In this second version of self-reintegration we take a more unconscious approach. The benefit of doing it this way is that it takes off a significant amount of conscious pressure for you to generate nominalizations and states cognitively. Another benefit is the fact that you know the pattern inside-out at this point, which means doing it cognitively may change the results because you consciously know what's coming next. Doing the reintegration hypnotically sidesteps any interference that would keep you from reaching a positive resolution. This pattern is also great if you actively use self-hypnosis and prefer to experience change through trance.

In the next section, we present some basic self-hypnosis techniques that you can use in order to generate trance for yourself. These techniques are easy to use even if you do not have a background in self-hypnosis. If you do have a standard self-hypnosis practice and easily drop into deep trance, then feel free to move on to the following section where we begin to explore the ways in which you can use the Visual Squash while in trance.

Self-Hypnosis

Technique One

This first technique involves using self-talk and imagery to create a hypnotic state. Begin by placing your feet flat on the floor and rest your hands on your lap. With your eyes open or closed, move your awareness to your right arm. While focusing your attention there, repeat to yourself, "My right arm is relaxing." Complete this three times and then shift your awareness to your left arm and repeat. After both arms are relaxed, focus on your right leg — "My right leg is relaxing" — and then your left leg: "My left leg is relaxing."

Next, allow your awareness to rest on your breathing and repeat to yourself three times, "My breathing is easy and comfortable." Now shift your attention to your heartbeat and repeat to yourself, "My heartbeat is regular and easy." Spend a few moments experiencing your heartbeat. At first it may be a kinesthetic sensation of a beating in your chest but perhaps it develops into you being able to hear the beat of your own heart. The more you rest your awareness there, the easier it becomes to hear your own heartbeat. This has a profound effect on your state.

Now it is time to engage the visual part of your processing. Scan your body and notice the relaxation and comfort. As you experience this, what color comes to mind? Notice the color representing the relaxation and comfort you are experiencing. As you do that you may notice some parts of you not yet experiencing that color. If you do, imagine sending that wave of relaxation, that color, to those parts of you. Continue this process until that color of comfort has circulated through you completely.

You may choose to deepen the trance at this stage. One way of doing this is to imagine standing at the top of a staircase and beginning to walk down. Each step can take you deeper into trance. Notice how the steps feel, what they are made of, their color, and your surroundings. That staircase can have as many steps as needed for you to enjoy a profoundly deep and comfortable trance.

Another way to deepen the trance is through fractionation. *Fractionation* is bringing yourself out of trance slightly and then dropping back down into it. The more you fractionate the trance, the deeper it becomes. You can do this by opening your eyes on each count, as you count backwards from 50. On each number, you can close your eyes then open them again. For example, count

50, then close your eyes. Open your eyes before counting 49, and when you count 49, then close your eyes again. Continue this process until your eyes want to remain comfortably closed.

Technique Two

If you are skilled at going into trance and experiencing hypnotic phenomena, then you may enjoy this induction. The idea here is that you can use hypnotic phenomena as the induction itself. Sitting with your feet flat on the floor and your hands resting on your lap, choose one hand to be your trance hand. Next, choose one finger on that hand to be your trance finger. Send your awareness to that finger and repeat in your mind, "My finger is getting lighter, my finger is moving." Use your best hypnotic tonality. Think these words to yourself as if you were presenting them verbally to a client. You may even choose to hear the words in someone else's voice, someone with whom you have strong hypnotic rapport. As you're hearing those words giving suggestions regarding your awareness in that hand, or in that finger, you may begin to notice some changes happening. If you're watching that finger you may begin to see tiny ideomotor movements. If your eyes are closed you will feel them.

Once you have the movement, you have trance, or at the very least unconscious cooperation with the process. Once this movement has begun you can continue with positive self-suggestion for comfort, relaxation, and a deepening of the experience. Depending on how much you have developed your hypnotic ability, this process may be very quick or may take a little longer. The more you practice it, though, the easier it becomes, so that eventually when you set out with the intention of going into trance it is simply the intention that will trigger the trance. You will not need the induction process.

Any method that you choose for self-hypnosis will work. The purpose here is to provide you with some techniques that you can use. Explore the power of your mind by experimenting with these techniques and other versions of self-hypnosis until you find the formula you best.

Hypnotic Self-Reintegration

Now that you have entered a comfortable trance we can

begin the process of reintegrating both parts. While in trance we tend to be far more associative, so this process might happen quickly as you will be far more sensitive to the subtle shifts in your state.

To begin, start with the more positive part. Unlike the other versions of the Visual Squash where we look for symbols, this time your symbol will be the actual experience of the part. As you think about the positive part, either think of the last time and place you experienced it, or if you have not experienced it yet, imagine what it would be like to be in that situation. While you are in this part, notice what you're seeing, hearing, feeling, and any other details that will be significant. As you associate into the positive part, become aware of your feelings. These feelings are what we will be chunking up. Just as in the previous version, you are looking for the state shift. Something to keep in mind as you go forward is that you may have a strong state shift as you associate into each part of this experience.

The question to ask yourself then is, "Is the state sustainable?" This once again goes back to the issue of end state energy. When you associate in, for example, you may have a sudden jolt of excitement. Excitement is a wonderful resource, however, it is not sustainable for an extended period of time. When this happens, be curious about what positive state lies just beyond it. As you begin to move through the states it is not important whether you consciously connect a nominalization or label to it or not. We are using the associative experience, the emotion, as our chunk for finding the highest positive intention.

Once you have explored the positive end state energy, it is time to move to the conflicting part. Because you are in the unique position of understanding this pattern and how parts, emotions, and problems work, the chunking up will be fairly easy. You may find at first there is an emotional state that is problematic or distinctly conflicting. Just as in the positive side, keep in mind you're looking for the end state energy. A negative state or an emotion that leaves you feeling less than resourceful is not a useful state to maintain. You can then ask your unconscious what is on the other side of that state. You may feel yourself actually moving through states as if you were moving through space, especially if you're in a deeper trance.

The reintegration is going to use even less conscious involvement. Unlike the cognitive version of the Visual Squash, you may not have any conscious awareness about the skills that will be coming from both sides. Instead, because your unconscious mind is close to the surface, you just need to set the intention for a skills exchange. This means knowing that both parts have skills and allowing the unconscious to exchange the skills on each side of the conflict. You may ask the unconscious mind to do it, or you can just comfortably know that it's taking place. This is an interesting experience because you might find that you have kinesthetic sensations associated with it. You may have a sense of something moving from one side of you to another. Your unconscious mind may also give you visual representations of this happening. Perhaps your unconscious mind will provide a symbolic representation of the transfer that's taking place. It could be some image connecting both sides of the problem or perhaps pictures moving from one side to the other. In whatever way your unconscious mind chooses to make this process known to your conscious awareness, you can rest comfortably, knowing there is a change taking place.

The last part of this integration is to unify both parts at the unconscious level. We do this by imagining both parts, both situations, side-by-side, and allowing them to blend. Think of this as overlapping the images. This will have a very interesting effect on your mind. As both sides overlap, it becomes very difficult to distinguish either part clearly or to even make sense of the visual representation you are seeing. Once that occurs, allow the images to fade and your mind to drift.

Drifting is a very important part of the process. In fact, it is a valuable tool in most hypnotic processes. Allowing the unconscious mind and the conscious mind to drift opens the space for the new connections being made in your neurology. As your mind drifts through thoughts, feelings, and dreams, your unconscious mind will present you with a new symbol, a new representation of the unified you. You will know it when you feel the state shift that feels totally congruent with your end state energy. Enjoy this part of the process and take as much time as you need. When it is completed, you can bring yourself back in anyway that is comfortable for you. An easy way of doing this is to count from one to five in your mind. You can also go back up the steps that you originally walked down to deepen the trance, if you used that form of deepening.

It is always a nice gesture as well to take a few moments to thank your unconscious mind for the work it has done for you. This may seem like a trivial gesture considering that it is, well, *you*. However, you may be pleasantly surprised by the results that come from it. If you were to take a moment now to close your eyes and thank your unconscious mind for all of the positive changes it has made in your life, notice what happens. Did you see an image or notice a feeling? Did your state shift? Everyone likes to be appreciated. Appreciate *you* for everything that you have accomplished, all of the changes you've made, everything you have learned.

Receive your book bonus at www.visualsquashbookbonus.com

Chapter Thirteen: Conclusion

We would like to take a moment to thank the best parts of each of you for spending time learning and reading with us and throughout the entire journey you have made through the Visual Squash. It is our sincerest hope that you continue to experiment and explore all of the possibilities in negotiating between all of the different parts of you and the world around you. Like every NLP pattern, the success of the Visual Squash comes down to the energy you put into it, so enjoy exploring your own creativity and all of the ways that you can adapt the Visual Squash when working with clients, in business, or with yourself. This is only a sampling of the variety of ways in which you can use this pattern and develop your own variations of it.

You have had quite the journey through the NLP Visual Squash. You have mastered a number of coaching and hypnotic skills including symbol elicitation, catalepsy, and chunking. These skills are useful not just within this pattern but across many others as well.

You have also explored how you can use the Visual Squash in a number of different ways. Whether the situation calls for a conversational, content-free, or deep trance Squash, you are well prepared. Because you understand the principal structure of change, the Meta Pattern, you are in a wonderful position to create your own varieties of the Visual Squash as well as your own original patterns.

Finally you have the tools to use the Squash not just in coaching but also in business and with yourself. This pattern is incredibly versatile and can be applied in any setting where a negotiation is taking place. The Visual Squash ensures that you have a win-win result in your external and internal negotiations. You can even explore new ways to integrate the various parts of you that lead you to greater happiness, success, and well-being.

We certainly hope that you've enjoyed this process of learning and sharing your energy and time with us. When it comes to your clients, learning, and your own conscious and unconscious mind, stay curious and enjoy everything that curiosity will bring you.

Receive your book bonus at www.visualsquashbookbonus.com

Appendix: Developing Calibration Skills

As we have discussed throughout this book, having the ability to calibrate your client's states as well as their unconscious communications is a crucial part of the Visual Squash, and of coaching as a whole. In this section we share a couple of strategies for improving your calibration skills so that you will be able to spot even the tiniest state shift or communication. These strategies can be practiced both with clients and in your everyday interactions. As you practice, your calibration skills will dramatically improve.

BMIRs

BMIRs (Behavioral Manifestations of Internal Representations) are the connection between your thoughts and your physiology. Our bodies show the outside world how we are thinking and feeling. Typical BMIRs include, breathing rate, muscle tension or relaxation, skin color, and eye movements..

The question is, what is exactly should you be looking for? In a word, nothing! That is, if you are actively looking for something, you will miss most of the unconscious communication coming from your client. This is because you will most likely be using the wrong kind of vision for coaching. We will go into more depth about this a little bit later. For now, let's focus on the things you will be consciously and unconsciously noticing.

We all have filters, beliefs, values, and ideas that shape the way information is taken in through the senses. Once that information passes through those filters, we create an internal representation of it where we may distort, delete, or generalize the information. This simply means that we take external information and fit it to our internal map of the world. We may alter that information, exclude parts or all of it, or we may begin to apply it in other situations.

That internal representation then impacts our state. It leads us to have feelings or an internal experience. The state that we generate based on those feelings or that experience is then manifested physically in our behavior. Behavior, in this context, includes both conscious actions and unconscious physical responses.

Imagine someone being hypnotized. The hypnotist's words are first filtered through the client's ideas about what hypnosis is and what it might feel like (to name just a couple of filters). Next, those words begin to create an internal experience for the client that fits in with their map of the world. This leads to a change in the client's state. Perhaps they are experiencing comfort, peace, or are having an awareness of the developing trance. Finally, that state is manifested by the change in the client's breathing, their muscle relaxation, the change in their color, and the closing of their eyes.

These behavioral manifestations of internal representations, or BMIRs, are the keys that give us a picture of what is happening inside the client's mind. In the Visual Squash there's a number of BMIRs you could be looking out for. The first set is in how the client describes the conflict. You are looking for the ways they spatially delineate the two parts. You are also looking for the shifts in their physiology that indicate the problem and resource states. Throughout the Squash you may also notice BMIRs that indicate trance. All of the sensory information the client is giving you can be useful. Some of it you may use, other parts you may just make a note of, and with others you may do nothing at all.

So now you are back to the question: how do you look for these changes in behavior? During the coaching process, if you are actively looking for BMIRs, the odds are you will miss an awful lot. This is because when you actively look for something, you are utilizing a very specific type of vision, foveal, which uses the center of the eye. This type of vision is not the most useful for registering movement. Imagine ancient humans roaming through the jungle looking for food. A saber-toothed tiger approaches from their left side. If those humans were in foveal vision looking for food, they wouldn't register the tiger approaching, and they would have become dinner! Instead, humans are highly adaptive and those early jungle dwellers had a different way of looking. They expanded their vision in such a way that movement from the sides, in front, above and below, even behind them, could be registered. This is the type of vision we use to register BMIRs.

When working with clients, the best indicator of BMIRs is movement. We mean movement in the broadest sense. It may be twitches in fingers or tapping a foot but it also may include alterations in breathing, eye movements, changes in blush, and muscle relaxation. All of these can indicate something is happening inside of the client. The purpose here is not to make any judgments about what those movements may mean. We aren't reading minds here; we are simply noticing differences. For example, a client may tap their food during the intake and pretalk. Some may be inclined to interpret that as being a sign of impatience, nervousness, or something else negative. It may be that they are keeping a beat, or perhaps the movement is a habit. What would be of interest to us is to know at what points the tapping stops. The less time we spend interpreting, the more we can be aware of what is taking place in front of us.

For the rest of this chapter we present techniques that you can practice to develop your calibration skills to such a level that when you sit with a client, everything happens automatically and you need not even have a conscious awareness of it.

Sorting for Life

This is a wonderful technique for changing the way in which your brain is processing sensory information. Next time you are in a public place, or a room with other people in it, take a moment and make yourself comfortable. Begin with the intention that visually you will only register things that are living in your environment. This includes people, animals (if there are any), plants (if there are any), maybe even insects! Again, the only things of interest are those things that are alive. Everything else can move into the background. Your unconscious mind knows how to do this; we do it all the time. Think of the last time you watched a movie. You "sorted" for that film and everything else dropped out of your awareness. With this intention, begin scanning the room. You may notice something interesting start to happen. Some people described this as a darkening of everything that isn't alive so that the things that are alive are in a bubble of light. Others experience it as if there is a pushing of the things that are not alive into the background while those things that are alive come to the foreground.

Once you have that experience, refine it. Set the intention that you're sorting for human life. Human life is the most important element in your environment. As you scan your environment, notice what happens with the people versus everything else.

This is very useful because it cuts down significantly on the visual interference that can come into play when working with clients.

The Coaching State

Sorting for life is the first step. We now need a way to access the right type of vision and the right type of state inside of us in order to be open to the tiniest of movements. When a client changes states, there is movement. It may be a movement of the limbs, however, more often than not it is a change in the their breathing, their heart rate, their eyes, or their skin tone. Being able to discern these types of movement will make you incredibly influential as a coach.

The exercise I'm about to describe will help you to access the ideal state for coaching. This state involves the quieting of your conscious processes so that your unconscious mind can be free to notice the client's unconscious communication as well as interact with that client both consciously and unconsciously.

Sit comfortably and find a spot on the wall in front of you that you can focus your gaze on. If you have a corner of a picture or some other edge, that may be easier. As you gaze at that point, imagine you can see the tiniest point in that spot. You can see the variances in color, the differences in light and shadow, and it's as if you could see the tiny molecules that make up that point. Allow your gaze to narrow so intensely that it feels like you could see right through that point.

Now allow your vision to relax. You can still see that spot

but you can see the rest of the wall in front of you. Still looking at that spot, begin to see what's to your right and what's to your left. As you see what's to your sides and that wall in front of you, you can have a sense of the space in front of you and the space behind you. Notice the sounds coming from your left, right, in front of you, behind you, above you, and below you. You can even have a sense of the space above you and the space below you.

With this expansive consciousness, imagine that you can wrap your awareness around you. If you are working with a client, wrap your expanded awareness around them. It is almost like creating a "coaching bubble."

From this state, imagine how easy it will be to work with clients, seeing everything that they're communicating. This exercise is incredibly useful because it activates your peripheral vision. This does a couple of different things. It accesses your parasympathetic nervous system, your relaxation response. That is an incredibly resourceful state for you to be in when working with clients. It also cuts down on any self-talk you may be experiencing. Finally, because you are accessing peripheral vision, it becomes much easier to register movement. This is a skill that is been programmed into us through thousands and thousands of years of evolution. Remember our ancient relatives in the jungle with the tiger? When you are in peripheral vision, you're able to discern movement with greater ease.

Enjoy practicing both of these exercises time and again so that your unconscious mind begins to do this automatically. The more you practice, the easier it becomes. A client will walk in and you have the intention of accessing the coaching state, and it will develop. You can also enjoy practicing these outside of the coaching context. You may be surprised at all the things that you will notice in your environment and your interactions that you had not noticed before now.

About the Authors

Jess Marion is a trainer with the International Center for Positive Change and Hypnosis and founder and director of Philadelphia Hypnosis. She is a NLP/HNLP and hypnosis trainer, NLP/HNLP Master Practitioner, and consulting hypnotist. Jess runs a busy private practice in Philadelphia and lives and works in New York and Philadelphia.

Shawn Carson is founder and co-director of the International Center for Positive Change and Hypnosis. He is an NLP/HNLP and hypnosis trainer and he runs a thriving training center in New York City. Shawn is a consulting hypnotist and works with private clients for trance-formational change. Originally from the UK, Shawn now lives in Manhattan, New York.

Acknowledgments

First and foremost, we are indebted to the co-founders of NLP, Richard Bandler and John Grinder, without whom nobody would be practicing in this wonderful discipline.

We would like to thank John Overdurf who, directly or indirectly, taught us everything we truly understand about NLP. John stands as a shining example of a self-examined life. We stand in awe of John's compassion and skill, and truly believe that he is "doing it right."

We'd like to thank our hypnosis teachers, Melissa Tiers of the Center for Integrative Hypnosis in New York City, and Igor Ledochowski from streethypnosis.com. In our model of the world, NLP and hypnosis are two sides of the same coin; you cannot properly practice one without the other. Melissa and Igor taught us what trance is.

We would like to thank our wonderful editor, Nancy Rawlinson, for her hard work and patience.

Finally, we would like to thank our business partner, Shawn's lovely wife Sarah, for her invaluable support and suggestions.

Glossary

Anchor: An external stimulus such as a touch that you feel, a gesture or image that you see, or word or sound that you hear, which leads you to feel a certain emotional state.

BMIRs: Behavioral Manifestations of Internal Representations

Catalepsy: A balancing of the muscles that indicates an unconscious process is taking place.

Chunking Up: Moving an experience from the sensory level to higher levels of abstraction.

Coach: Someone leading another person through a process of change, for example by using the Swish Pattern.

Collapsing Anchors: Activating two anchors simultaneously so that one anchor is neutralized.

HNLP: Humanistic Neuro-Linguistic Psychology.

Logical Levels: The ways we organize our experience through environment, behaviors, capabilities, beliefs, values, identity, and beyond identity.

Meta Pattern: The structure of all change beginning with the problem state, moving to a neutral state, and then into the resource state. The resource state is then brought back to the problem.

Synesthesia: An overlapping of representation systems, such as when you hear a word and have a feeling.

VAK: An acronym of the major kinds of sensory information: visual, auditory, and kinesthetic

Value: An auditory digital (self-talk) positive kinesthetic synesthesia.

Other Books from the Authors

Quit: The Hypnotist's Handbook to Running Effective Stop Smoking Sessions

By Jess Marion, Sarah Carson, and Shawn Carson

Forward by Igor Ledochowski

NLP Mastery Series: The Swish

By Shawn Carson and Jess Marion

Forward by John Overdurf

Keeping the Brain in Mind: Practical Neuroscience for Coaches, Therapists, and Hypnosis Practitioners

By: Shawn Carson and Melissa Tiers

Forward by: Dr. Lincoln Bickford M.D., Ph.D.